# 1500 BIBLE QUIZZES

# 1500
# BIBLE QUIZZES

# Great Bible Sayings in
# Question and Answer Form

By
Amos R. Wells

LONDON
PICKERING & INGLIS LTD

PICKERING & INGLIS LTD
29 LUDGATE HILL, LONDON EC4M 7BP
26 BOTHWELL STREET, GLASGOW G2 6PA


Reprinted 1969 by
Baker Book House Company


Copyright, 1931, by
W. A. Wilde Company


ISBN 0 7208 0309 8

Cat. No. 01/0615


*First printing 1968*
*Second printing 1971*
*Third printing 1973*
*This British edition 1974*


This edition is issued by
special arrangements with
BAKER BOOK HOUSE
the American publishers


Printed in Great Britain by
Lowe & Brydone (Printers) Ltd, Thetford, Norfolk

# PREFACE

No gold mine in the world, nor all the world's gold mines together, can compare in riches with the sayings of the Bible.

This book brings the greatest and best-known of those sayings together,—fifteen hundred of them.

If you will become familiar with these fifteen hundred sentences, you will possess yourself of the soul of the Bible.

You will gain its wit and wisdom, you will have its practical sagacity and its insight into spiritual things. You will come to know God and Christ and to dwell with the Holy Spirit. You will obtain courage for the trials of earth and a happy place in the mansions of heaven.

The Bible contains 31,173 verses. This book has selected one-twentieth of these. It is too much to say that it includes all the most memorable, but it does include probably all that one is likely to meet in ordinary references, in reading or speech. Learning these fifteen hundred verses will give you a substantial working knowledge of the Bible.

The question-and-answer form has been chosen as the most vivacious and practical, and pains have been taken to vary the questions so as to prevent monotony.

For private use, spaces are left for the copying of the answers from the back of the book, if that is desired; but it is better not to do this, but to keep at it till the answers leap to your mind at once in reply to the questions.

For use in the home or in a Sunday-school class, one person will give out the questions and keep a record of the success or failure of the answers. At first it will be well to accept incomplete or vague replies, but after a while increased accuracy should be re-

3

quired until the verses can be repeated just as they stand in the Bible, word by word.

After a while you may add to the study the names of the books where the different verses are found, then the chapters, and some of you may be able to go on to the verse numbers. Your great-great-grandparents had no difficulty even with the last feat.

I have used the King James version rather than any of the later translations, because it is the version used by the vast majority of persons, and quite universally quoted in literature.

One caution. Do not allow yourself to be discouraged. At first you will be dismayed to find how little of the Bible you actually know, with anything approaching accuracy. You may go through an entire series of twenty-five questions and not be able to answer one of them, though pains have been taken to intersperse the most familiar verses with those less familiar.

But persevere. It is well worth while. The second time you go over a series of questions you will be able to answer more of them, and so with every time you review them, until by and by you will be letter perfect; and then what joy and pride and enrichment!

While putting this book together I wrote the following verses, which may serve as a concluding bit of stimulus for the study:

## WHO SAID?

Who said, "Blessed are the mourners"?
   Who said, "Happy are the poor"?
Who declared himself the Shepherd?
   Who declared himself the Door?
Who, when tempests darkly lower,
   Is the Dayspring of the day?
Who, in all our tangled courses,
   Names himself the Living Way?

4

# BIBLE SAYINGS

Whose the saying, "God is light"?
  Whose the saying, "God is love"?
Who commanded, "Set your heart
  On the things that are above"?
Who compared the tongue to fire?
  Who compared God's grace to snow?
Who compared to growing light
  Paths whereon God's people go?

Who said, "The Lord my Shepherd is"?
  Who said, "My Tower he"?
Who said, "He is my Strength and Song
  And evermore shall be"?
Who said, "The Lord my God is good,
  His blessings aye endure,
And all his glorious promises
  Are lasting and secure"?

"Who said—?" Behold, a mirror shows
  Redoubled what is fair,
And all the world of loveliness
  Increases glory there.
So words and speaker, let them live
  Together in our mind,
Each in the other's beauteousness
  An echoing joy to find.

*Auburndale, Mass.*

AMOS R. WELLS

# BIBLE SAYINGS

## SERIES I

1. Who said, "Is not this great Babylon, that I have built"?........
..............................................................................................
2. Finish Christ's sentence, "These ought ye to have done, and not—." ..............................................................................
3. Who said, "Days should speak, and multitude of years should teach wisdom"?..............................................................
4. Who promised his people, "The Lord shall fight for you, and ye shall hold your peace"?.......................................................
5. What is the verse of the Psalm that ends, "all ye lands"?........
..............................................................................................
6. Who said, "Thou shalt have joy and gladness; and many shall rejoice at his birth"? To whom was it said, and of whom? ..............................................................................
7. In what Book is the saying about the Lamb's book of life?........
..............................................................................................
8. Who advised the Sanhedrin to let the Christians alone, saying that if their work was of God, it could not be overthrown?
9. Who said, "Therefore shall a man leave his father and his mother, and shall cleave unto his wife"?..............................
10. What is Christ's saying which begins, "If the Son therefore shall make you free—"?..........................................................
11. Who commanded, "Breach for breach, eye for eye, tooth for tooth"? ..............................................................................
12. What did James say no man could tame?...................................
13. Finish Paul's sentence, "The goodness of God leadeth—."........
..............................................................................................
14. What is the rest of Christ's saying, "This kind can come forth by nothing, but—"?..............................................................
15. Who wrote, "Looking for that blessed hope, and the glorious appearing of the great God and our Saviour Jesus Christ"?........
..............................................................................................

16. Who praised the man that "sweareth to his own hurt, and changeth not"? .................................................................................

17. Who exhorted his people, "Be not ye afraid of them: remember the Lord, which is great and terrible, and fight for your brethren, your sons, and your daughters, your wives, and your houses"? .....................................................................

18. In what Book is the saying, "Many waters cannot quench love"? ...........................................................................................

19. Who said, "This is my beloved Son, in whom I am well pleased"? On what occasion?..........................................

20. Who speaks about "Redeeming the time, because the days are evil"? .........................................................................................

21. Who said, "The isles shall wait for his law"?..........................

22. What proverb ends with "how good it is!"? ...........................

23. Finish the sentence, "Eye hath not seen, nor ear heard, neither have entered into the heart of man—.".................................

24. Who said that in the judgment day a man shall give account of every idle word he has spoken?.........................................

25. Complete Paul's saying, "This is the will of God, even—.".......... ..........................................................................................................

## SERIES II

1. What is the rest of the proverb, "My son, if sinners entice thee—"? ...............................................................................

2. Whose is the saying about the axe laid to the root of the trees? ..........................................................................................................

3. Who said of the religious leaders of his day that they said "Peace, peace," when there was no peace?...................................

4. What did Paul call "the first commandment with promise"? ..........................................................................................................

5. Who asked God to put his tears into his bottle?.........................

6. Who laid his sin to "the woman whom thou gavest to be with me"? ...............................................................................................

8

# BIBLE SAYINGS

7. Who said of God that he is "of purer eyes than to behold evil," and that he cannot look on iniquity?......................................

8. Of whom did Christ say that they loved "the uppermost seats in the synagogues"?......................................

9. What is the proverb about spreading a net in the sight of a bird? ......................................

10. To whom did God say, "The Lord searcheth all hearts"?..........

11. Who said, "Behold the handmaid of the Lord; be it unto me according to thy word"?......................................

12. Finish Paul's saying, "The natural man receiveth not—"?........

......................................

13. What is the first part of the sentence which ends, "and into his courts with praise"?......................................

14. Of whom was it asked in astonishment whether he also was among the prophets?......................................

15. Of whom did the Lord ask, "Who is this that darkeneth counsel by words without knowledge?"......................................

16. Finish the quotation from Isaiah: "I will say to the north, Give up; and to the south, Keep not back."......................................

17. What is Christ's question about spoiled salt?......................................

18. Finish the quotation, "In that he himself hath suffered being tempted—." ......................................

19. What is the rest of the verse in Deuteronomy beginning, "If from thence thou shalt seek the Lord thy God—"?......................................

20. What saying of Christ's concerning his pre-existence introduces Abraham? ......................................

21. What is Paul's saying about "respect of persons"?......................................

22. What is the proverb about pride and a fall?......................................

23. Finish the promise in Leviticus, "Ye shall lie down—."..............

......................................

24. In what Book is the prayer, "Lead me to the rock that is higher than I"?......................................

25. Who said to a mighty king, "Let thy gifts be to thyself, and give thy rewards to another"?......................................

# BIBLE SAYINGS

## SERIES III

1. To whom did the Lord say, "Speak unto the children of Israel, that they go forward"?.....................

2. In whose song are the words, "He hath put down the mighty from their seats, and exalted them of low degree"?..................

3. What is Paul's saying contrasting the letter and the spirit?....
.....................................................

4. Finish Peter's saying, "One day is with the Lord as a thousand years—." .....................................

5. What is the rest of the saying, "Better is it that thou shouldest not vow—." .....................................

6. In what Book is the great affirmation, "Hear, O Israel: The Lord our God is one Lord"?.....................

7. Who asked the question, "Shall we receive good at the hand of God, and shall we not receive evil?".....................

8. What proverb about grapes did Ezekiel refute?.....................
.....................................................

9. Who did Christ say are his brother, his sister, and his mother? .....................................

10. Finish Paul's sentence, "Ye are all the children of God—."......
.....................................................

11. Give the sentence from the Revelation which ends, "and their works do follow them.".....................

12. To what does the proverb compare pleasant words?..............
.....................................................

13. Finish the words of the Psalm, "My soul, wait thou only upon God; for—.".....................

14. To whom was it said, "Dust thou art, and unto dust shalt thou return"? .....................................

15. Complete the warcry, "The sword of the Lord—.".....................

16. Who said, "We will give ourselves continually to prayer, and to the ministry of the word"?.....................

# BIBLE SAYINGS

17. Who said of marriage, "What therefore God hath joined together, let not man put asunder"?......................................
18. Finish the verse of the Psalm, "O thou that hearest prayer—." ....................................................................................
19. Who said, "I am doing a great work, so that I cannot come down"? ............................................................................
20. Finish the proverb, "Trust in the Lord with all thy heart; and—." ...................................................................................
21. To what did Paul compare the coming of "the day of the Lord"? ..............................................................................
22. Of whom is it said in Hebrews that of them "the world was not worthy"? .......................................................................
23. What is the saying in Hosea about being "joined to idols"?....
24. What command follows "Cease to do evil"? Who said it?....
.....................................................................................................
25. What is Christ's saying about the coming night?......................

## SERIES IV

1. What is the rest of Paul's question, "Thou therefore which teachest another,—"?......................................................
2. Who said, "If I perish, I perish"?............................................
3. What proverb begins, "In all thy ways acknowledge him—"?
4. Who said, "Know ye not that there is a prince and a great man fallen this day in Israel?" Of whom was he speaking?....
.....................................................................................................
5. What is Christ's saying about confessing him before men?....
.....................................................................................................
6. Finish the verse of the Psalm, "Thou crownest the year with thy goodness."..................................................................
7. Who sung, "Who is like unto thee, O Lord, among the gods? Who is like thee, glorious in holiness, fearful in praises, doing wonders"? On what occasion?......................................

11

# BIBLE SAYINGS

8. Finish this sentence from Habakkuk: "Woe to him that buildeth a town with blood—.".....................................................
9. After opening the eyes of the man blind from birth, what did Christ say about himself?.....................................................
10. Complete the command, "Exhort one another daily—."...........
.......................................................................................................

11. Who wrote, "The fruit of righteousness is sown in peace of them that make peace"?.....................................................
12. Through whom did God promise Israel, "I have blotted out, as a thick cloud thy transgressions, and, as a cloud, thy sins"?
13. Finish the sentence of the Psalm, "The Lord is merciful and gracious—." ...................................................................................
14. Who said, "I dwell among mine own people"?...........................
15. Who said, "I have planted, Apollos watered; but God gave the increase"?.....................................................
16. Who said of death, "There the wicked cease from troubling; and there the weary be at rest"?.....................................................
17. Who said, "This is my beloved Son, in whom I am well pleased"? Of whom did he speak? When?..............................
18. Finish Paul's words, "It is good to be zealously affected—."....
.......................................................................................................

19. Who said of Moses that he was "learned in all the wisdom of the Egyptians, and was mighty in words and in deeds"?..........
20. Complete the proverb, "The hoary head is a crown of glory, if—." ...............................................................................................
21. Who wrote, "The harvest is past, the summer is ended, and we are not saved"?.....................................................
22. What two masters did Christ say we cannot serve?....................
23. In what Book is Christ reported as calling himself "Alpha and Omega, the first and the last"?.....................................................
24. Whose are the words, "Thou art weighed in the balances, and art found wanting"? To what king were they addressed?........
25. "As far as the east is from the west—"; finish the sentence.....
.......................................................................................................

# BIBLE SAYINGS

## SERIES V

1. Finish the sentence, "Ye have not yet resisted unto blood—."
2. Who said, "The Most High dwelleth not in temples made with hands"? ...................................................................................................
3. Who asked, "Am I my brother's keeper?"...................................
4. Of whom was it said, when he died at the age of one hundred and twenty, "His eye was not dim, nor his natural force abated"? ...................................................................................................
5. Complete the prayer, "Create in me a clean heart, O God—."
6. Finish Christ's saying, "Suffer the little children—.".................
   ...................................................................................................
7. Who said, "I am he that liveth, and was dead; and, behold, I am alive for evermore"?.....................................................................
8. Finish the proverb, "Whom the Lord loveth—."............................
9. Who said, "The half was not told me," and concerning whom?
   ...................................................................................................
10. Fill out the verse, "In thy presence—," "at thy right hand."....
    ...................................................................................................
11. Complete Christ's question, "Is not the life more than meat—."
12. Who said, "Let God be true, but every man a liar"?.................
13. Who asked, "Is there no balm in Gilead; is there no physician there?" ...................................................................................................
14. Who spoke of the time "when the morning stars sang to-gether, and all the sons of God shouted for joy"? To whom did he speak? ...................................................................................................
15. Who asked, "Should such a man as I flee?"...............................
16. Who said, "One thing I know, that, whereas I was blind, now I see"? ...................................................................................................
17. What is the first part of the sentence ending "loadeth us with benefits"? ...................................................................................................
18. Who said, "My punishment is greater than I can bear"?........
    ...................................................................................................

19. Who wrote, "There is one God, and one mediator between God and men, the man Christ Jesus"?.............................

20. Who said, "Follow me, and I will make you fishers of men"? To whom?.............................

21. Who wrote, "Then shall we know, if we follow on to know the Lord"? .............................

22. Complete Christ's saying, "A man's life consisteth not—."........
.............................

23. Who wrote, "The soul that sinneth, it shall die"?.........................

24. Who received this commandment regarding the law of God: "Turn not from it to the right hand or to the left, that thou mayest prosper withersoever thou goest"?.............................

25. Complete this quotation from Habakkuk: "The earth shall be filled with the knowledge of the glory of the Lord—."...........
.............................

## SERIES VI

1. What verse of a psalm about zeal was quoted with reference to Christ?.............................

2. What verse in Hosea contrasts mercy and sacrifice?..................

3. What is the verse about God's love and his chastening?...............
.............................

4. What is the great saying about Enoch?.............................

5. Who said, "Woe unto him that striveth with his Maker!"........
.............................

6. Finish the proverb that says of wisdom, "Length of days is in her right hand—."............................

7. Who asked Christ the question, "Good Master, what shall I do that I may inherit eternal life?".............................

8. Complete Paul's sentence, "Where the spirit of the Lord is—."
.............................

9. What Book tells about "the song of Moses and the Lamb"?....
.............................

10. What is the rest of the prayer of David beginning, "O Lord, open thou my lips—"?.......................

11. Whose song begins, "Sing ye to the Lord, for he hath triumphed gloriously"?.......................

12. Who received the promise that, if he meditated on God's law, "then thou shalt make thy way prosperous, and then thou shalt have good success"?.......................

13. Who expressed the wish, "Oh that my head were waters, and mine eyes a fountain of tears!".......................

14. What prophet cried, "Woe unto him that giveth his neighbor drink"? .......................

15. Finish the Beatitude, "Blessed are the poor in spirit—.".......... . .......................

16. What is Paul's saying about "the yoke of bondage"?............... .......................

17. Of what occasion is it said, "So they read in the book in the law of God distinctly, and gave the sense, and caused them to understand the reading"?.......................

18. Of whose pursuit of the enemy is the phrase used, "Faint, yet pursuing"? .......................

19. What verse of a psalm speaks of God's pity of his children?.... .......................

20. In what parable is the expression, "Take thine ease, eat, drink, and be merry"?.......................

21. Finish Paul's saying, "In Jesus Christ neither circumcision availeth anything, nor uncircumcision; but—.".......................

22. Complete the saying in Job, "They that plow iniquity, and sow wickedness—." .......................

23. What prophet commanded, "Make you a new heart and a new spirit; for why will ye die"?.......................

24. What is Christ's saying about climbing up "some other way" into the sheepfold?.......................

25. What is the proverb about wisdom being "the principal thing"? .......................

# BIBLE SAYINGS

## SERIES VII

1. What is Christ's saying about the lilies of the field?...................
2. Finish Peter's sentence, "The Lord is not slack concerning his promise, as some men count slackness—."...........................
........................................................................................
3. What Bible heroine did King Ahasuerus promise half of his kingdom? ...........................................................
4. Finish the command in Deuteronomy: "Thou shalt love the Lord thy God with—."...........................................
5. What is the first part of the proverb which ends, "and a brother is born for adversity"?...........................................
6. Finish Hosea's sentence, "They have sown the wind—."...........
........................................................................................
7. What is Paul's saying concerning the Christian's breastplate and helmet?...........................................
8. What is Isaiah's saying about sins being as snow and as wool?
9. Who sung, "He hath filled the hungry with good things; and the rich he hath sent empty away"?...........................................
10. Who said, "There is none righteous, no, not one." "There is none that doeth good, no, not one"?...........................................
11. Finish the sentence, "Be not drunk with wine, wherein is excess; but—."...........................................
12. What is the psalm prayer that speaks of the apple of the eye?
........................................................................................
13. Who was bidden to fight when he heard "the sound of a going in the tops of the mulberry trees"?...........................................
14. Who said to the sea, "Hitherto shalt thou come, but no further: and here shall thy proud waves be stayed"?...............
15. Whose decree was "according to the law of the Medes and Persians, which altereth not"?...........................................
16. Finish Paul's sentence, "We are laborers together with God."
........................................................................................

16

# BIBLE SAYINGS

17. Complete the Beatitude, "Blessed are they that mourn—."........
......................................................................................................

18. Of whom did the children of Belial say, "How shall this man save us"?......................................................................................

19. Who said, "My spirit shall not always strive with man," and when? ...................................................................................

20. Who asked the question, "Is it well with the child?"...............

21. In what Book is it said, "The king himself is served by the field"? ....................................................................................

22. Who said, "Who hath ears to hear, let him hear"?...................

23. What is Paul's description of the house of God?......................
......................................................................................................

24. Who said, "All things come of thee, and of thine own have we given thee"?......................................................................

25. Finish the saying, "We are made partakers of Christ, if—."
......................................................................................................

## SERIES VIII

1. Finish the sentence in Hebrews beginning, "No chastening for the present seemeth to be joyous, but grievous—."...................
......................................................................................................

2. What king said to his subjects, "My little finger shall be thicker than my father's loins"?...................................................

3. Who said, "Ye ask, and receive not, because ye ask amiss"?

4. Who said, on starting on a journey, "Rise up, Lord, and let thine enemies be scattered"?......................................................

5. To what church did the Spirit send the message, "Thou hast left thy first love"?..................................................................

6. To whom did the Lord give the promise, "Five of you shall chase an hundred, and an hundred of you shall put ten thousand to flight"?..............................................................................

7. What description of the path of the just is in the Book of Proverbs? ...........................................................................................

17

8. Finish Isaiah's sentence, "Look unto me, and be ye saved—."
..............................................................................................................

9. What is the blessing of the meek?....................................

10. Finish Paul's sentence, "All have sinned—."................................

11. What is the proverb about a merry heart?........................

12. Who said of the power of Israel, "I will overturn, overturn, overturn it: and it shall be no more, until he come whose right it is, and I will give it him"?....................................

13. Who asked, "What shall be done unto the man whom the king delighteth to honor?"................................

14. Finish the sentence, "God, who commanded the light to shine out of darkness, hath shined in our hearts—."........................
..............................................................................................................

15. Of whom was it said at his birth, "What manner of child shall this be?"................................

16. Who prophesied, "They shall beat their swords into plowshares, and their spears into pruning hooks"?........................

17. Who said, "The joy of the Lord is your strength"?....................

18. Of whom was it said that he was "very meek, above all the men who were upon the face of the earth"?........................

19. Who was asked, "Canst thou bind the sweet influences of Pleiades, or loose the bands of Orion?"................................

20. Finish Christ's sentence, "Seek ye first the kingdom of God, and his righteousness—."................................

21. In what Book is the saying about Armageddon?........................

22. Who said of Christ that he "died for us, that, whether we wake or sleep, we should live together with him"?........................

23. Finish the verse of the psalm beginning, "The sacrifices of God are—."................................
..............................................................................................................

24. Of what did Moses speak when he said, "This is the bread which the Lord hath given you to eat"?........................

25. Who said, "The dayspring from on high hath visited us"?........
..............................................................................................................

# BIBLE SAYINGS

## SERIES IX

1. Finish Christ's saying, "Whosoever hath, to him shall be given, and he shall have more abundance: but—." ....................
................................................................................................

2. Complete Christ's saying, "I am the door: by me if any man enter in—." ................................................................................

3. What is the rest of the verse in the psalm beginning, "The mountains shall bring peace to the people—"? ...........................

4. Of what time was it said, "There were giants in the earth in those days"? ..........................................................................................

5. In what Book are the words, "To-day if ye will hear his voice, harden not your hearts"? .............................................................

6. Who said, "I see the heavens opened, and the Son of man standing on the right hand of God"? ..........................................

7. To whom did Christ say, "One thing thou lackest"? ..................
................................................................................................

8. What prophet said, "Ye have plowed wickedness, ye have reaped iniquity"? ..........................................................................

9. What does Ecclesiastes say about him "that loveth silver"? ....
................................................................................................

10. What verse of the psalms contains seven names for the Lord?

11. Who asked God, "Give me now wisdom and knowledge, that I may go out and come in before this people"? ...........................

12. What is Christ's promise for those "which do hunger and thirst after righteousness"? .................................................................

13. What is Paul's "foundation" saying? ..........................................

14. What is the proverb about keeping the heart? ...........................

15. Who asked in dismay, "How shall the ark of the Lord come to me"? ................................................................................

16. What saying about God's laws was the origin of the phylacteries? ..................................................................................................

17. Who said, "It is not in man that walketh to direct his steps"?
................................................................................................

19

18. What are Paul's directions for the training of children?........
......................................................................................................................
19. To what church did the Spirit say, "Be thou faithful unto death, and I will give thee a crown of life"?................................
20. In what words did God exhort Joshua to courage?....................
......................................................................................................................
21. Who said, "My God hath sent his angel, and hath shut the lions' mouths"?................................................................................
22. Who said, "Your Father knoweth that ye have need of these things"? ......................................................................................
23. Who said, "Great is the mystery of godliness"?..........................
24. What was Peter's prophecy of "new heavens and a new earth"? ..........................................................................................
25. What simile does the psalmist use to express the brevity of human life? ......................................................................................

## SERIES X

1. To what prophet was it said, "O thou man of God, there is death in the pot"?..........................................................................
2. Finish this quotation from Job: "Shall mortal man be more just than God?"..................................................................................
3. Complete this sentence from Habakkuk: "The Lord is in his holy temple—."..................................................................................
4. What is the Beatitude for the merciful?........................................
5. What is Paul's saying about the leaven?........................................
6. What is James's saying about humility?........................................
7. What is the proverb that urges independence?............................
8. What is the beginning of the verse of the psalm which ends, "he drew me out of many waters"?................................................
9. What king said to his subjects, "My father hath chastised you with whips, but I will chastise you with scorpions"?................
10. Who said, "Blessed are your eyes, for they see: and your ears, for they hear"?......................................................................................

11. Who wrote, "See that none render evil for evil unto any man; but ever follow that which is good"?......................................

12. Who said, "There shall not be a man put to death this day: for to-day the Lord hath wrought salvation in Israel"?............

.........................................................................................................

13. Finish the quotation, "Lift up the hands which hang down."

.........................................................................................................

14. Who said, "Whatsoever cometh forth of the doors of my house to meet me, when I return in peace from the children of Ammon, shall surely be the Lord's, and I will offer it up for a burnt offering"?......................................

15. What was Isaiah's promise to the aged?......................................

16. Who cried in death, "Lord Jesus, receive my spirit"?............

17. In what parable are the words, "Yet hath he not root in himself"? .........................................................................................................

18. Finish the proverb, "Even a fool, when he holdeth his peace—." .........................................................................................................

19. Who said, "While the earth remaineth, seed time and harvest, and cold and heat, and summer and winter, and day and night shall not cease"? When was it said?......................................

20. Who asked of his people, "Whose ox have I taken? or whose ass have I taken? or whom have I defrauded? whom have I oppressed? or of whose hand have I received any bribe?"........

.........................................................................................................

21. In what Book is the song, "Alleluia: for the Lord God omnipotent reigneth"?......................................

22. Who said of Christ that he "was delivered for our offences, and was raised again for our justification"?......................................

23. Finish this verse of the psalm, "The mercy of the Lord is from everlasting to everlasting—."......................................

24. Of what substance is it said, "He that gathered much had nothing over, and he that gathered little had no lack"?............

25. Complete the quotation, "There is a spirit in man: and—."....

.........................................................................................................

# BIBLE SAYINGS

## SERIES XI

1. Finish this sentence from Hosea: "I drew them with cords of a man—.".................................................................

2. Complete Christ's saying: "I am the good shepherd—."...........
...................................................................................................

3. What Book contains the saying about the white stone and the new name?...............................................................................

4. Who said to his priests, "Ye shall stand still in Jordan"?........
...................................................................................................

5. Finish this verse from the psalm: "The Lord hath prepared his throne in the heavens."...............................................................

6. What is Christ's saying about taking thought for the morrow?
...................................................................................................

7. What is Paul's saying about "every creature of God"?...............
...................................................................................................

8. Who said, "We saw the children of Anak there"?....................

9. Who said, "Thou art a God ready to pardon, gracious and merciful, slow to anger, and of great kindness"?.......................

10. What is the Beatitude of the pure in heart?.............................
...................................................................................................

11. What was Paul's statement of the test of one's work?...............
...................................................................................................

12. Of whom was it said that they "out of weakness were made strong"? .....................................................................................

13. In what Book is it said of God's laws, "Thou shalt write them upon the posts of thy house, and on the gates"?.......................

14. Who has said, "There is no God"?.............................................

15. What is the conclusion of Habakkuk's sentence, "Although the fig tree shall not blossom, neither shall fruit be in the vines; the labor of the olive shall fail, and the fields shall yield no meat; the flock shall be cut off from the fold, and there shall be no herd in the stalls—"?...................................................

16. What is the conclusion of the parable of the rich fool?............

.................................................................................................

17. What is the end of James' sentence, "Resist the devil, and—"?

.................................................................................................

18. Who was tested by his pronunciation of Shibboleth?................

19. Whose was the urging, "Come ye, and let us walk in the light
of the Lord"?............

20. What was Christ's saying about trust in riches?................

.................................................................................................

21. Who said "Rejoice evermore"?................

22. Who asked "Can the Ethiopian change his skin, or the leopard
his spots?"............

23. Finish this sentence from Job: "Wrath killed the foolish
man—." ............

24. Complete this saying from Ecclesiastes: "When goods increase—." ............

25. Who cried, as he was stoned to death, "Lord, lay not this sin
to their charge"?............

## SERIES XII

1. Of whom is it said, "There was no room for them in the inn"?
2. Who said to God, "Behold, heaven and the heaven of heavens
cannot contain thee; how much less this house which I have
built!"? ............
3. To whom did God say, "Whoso sheddeth man's blood, by man
shall his blood be shed"?............
4. What promise in the psalms for "the poor of the people"?....

.................................................................................................

5. What is the proverb about the ant?............

.................................................................................................

6. Finish Paul's saying, "We faint not; for though our outward
man perish—."............

7. Who wrote, "God is light, and in him is no darkness at all"?

8. Who said, "Am I God, to kill and to make alive?" and on what occasion? ...................................................................

9. To what prophet was it said, "Son of man, I take away from thee the desire of thine eyes with a stroke"?....................................

10. What is Christ's saying about judging others?............................

11. Finish Paul's saying, "All the law is fulfilled in one word, even in this—.".................................................................

12. Who said to God, "I have heard of thee by the hearing of the ear, but now mine eye seeth thee"?....................................

13. Of whom was it said that the Lord blessed his house because of the ark of God?......................................................

14. What is the eyeservice verse in Ephesians?................................ ..

15. What is the Beatitude for the peacemakers?................................
...................................................................

16. What verse of the psalm is about a candle?................................

17. Who raised the warcry, "To your tents, O Israel"?....................

18. Who commanded, "Pray without ceasing"?................................

19. In what Book is God called "the Ancient of days"?....................
...................................................................

20. Finish the sentence from Hebrews: "They could not enter in—." ...................................................................

21. Who said of Canaan, "Let us go up at once, and possess it; for we are well able to overcome it"?....................................

22. Finish the verse from the psalm: "Who is God save the Lord?"
...................................................................

23. Finish Christ's sentence, "As the Father knoweth me—.".........
...................................................................

24. What is Paul's great verse about justification by faith?............
...................................................................

25. In what Book are the words, "The Lord thy God in the midst of thee is mighty; he will save, he will rejoice over thee with joy; he will rest in his love, he will joy over thee with singing"? ...................................................................

24

# BIBLE SAYINGS

## SERIES XIII

1. Of whom is it said that he "danced before the Lord with all his might"?..................................................................................
2. What is the Beatitude for the persecuted?....................................
3. What is Paul's saying about our being God's temple?...............

..................................................................................................
4. In what Book is the prophecy, "Many of them that sleep in the dust of the earth shall awake, some to everlasting life, and some to shame and everlasting contempt"?.................................
5. Finish Christ's saying, "Fear not, little flock—."........................
6. In what Book is the saying, "Blessed are they which are called unto the marriage supper of the Lamb"?...............................
7. Complete the verse from Isaiah: "The lofty looks of man shall be humbled, and the haughtiness of men shall be bowed down—." ..........................................................................................
8. Who asked, "Why is the house of God forsaken?"....................
9. What is Christ's saying about the needle's eye?.........................
10. Of whom was it falsely said, "This man is the great power of God"?...........................................................................................
11. What is the proverb about the sleep of the sluggard?...............
12. Who said, "Now I know that the Lord is greater than all gods," and when did he say it?................................................
13. Finish the saying in Job, "Man is born unto trouble, as—."....

..................................................................................................
14. Complete Paul's sentence, "With good will doing service—."

..................................................................................................
15. What is Christ's saying about his "other sheep"?.......................
16. Finish Job's sentence, "Cursed be the man that trusteth in man, and maketh flesh his arm—."..................................................
17. What is the rainbow verse of Genesis?.........................................
18. What is Paul's saying about walking in the Spirit?....................

..................................................................................................

# BIBLE SAYINGS

19. What did John say about the result of walking in the light?....
...................................................................................................
20. What did Paul say about earthen vessels?.................................
21. Complete the sentence, "The heavens declare the glory of God—." ...................................................................................
22. Finish the proverb: "The name of the Lord is a strong tower—." ...................................................................................
23. Who said, "Lord, it is nothing with thee to help, whether with many, or with them that have no power"?................................
24. Where is the verse, "There is no peace, saith the Lord, unto the wicked"?...................................................................................
25. To whom did an angel say, "I bring you good tidings of great joy, which shall be to all people"?.......................................

## SERIES XIV

1. What is Christ's saying about "the deceitfulness of riches"?
2. Who said, "In everything give thanks, for this is the will of God in Christ Jesus concerning you"?.................................
3. To what prophet did God say, if he prophesied faithfully, "Thou hast delivered thy soul"?....................................................
4. What is the verse of the psalm about rain on the mown grass?
5. What Book did Christ quote when he answered Satan, "Ye shall not tempt the Lord your God"?.............................................
6. What is Christ's saying about the mote and the beam?............
...................................................................................................
7. What is Paul's saying about bodily exercise?............................
8. Who said, "My father, if the prophet had bid thee do some great thing, wouldest thou not have done it?".............................
...................................................................................................
9. What does Ecclesiastes say about a workingman's sleep?........
...................................................................................................
10. To whom did the Lord say, "I bare you on eagles' wings, and brought you unto myself"?..............................................................

11. What is the origin of the saying, "What mean these stones?"

............................................................................................

12. To what church did the Spirit say, "Thou hast a name that thou livest, and art dead"?...............................................................

13. In what Book is the sentence, "The trees of the Lord are full of sap"?................................................................................

14. Who proposed the riddle, "Out of the eater came forth meat, and out of the strong came forth sweetness"?...........................

15. Finish the verse of the psalm, "He shall have dominion also from sea to sea—."...................................................................

16. Who called his followers "the salt of the earth"?........................

............................................................................................

17. Finish the verse in Hebrews, "There remaineth therefore a rest—."

18. Who received from God the command, "Thou shalt drink of the brook, and I have commanded the ravens to feed thee there"? ...............................................................................

19. In what Book is the command, "Follow peace with all men, and holiness, without which no man shall see the Lord"?........

............................................................................................

20. Complete the saying of the psalm: "O Lord, how manifold are thy works!"...................................................................

............................................................................................

21. What is Christ's saying about our treasure?..............................

............................................................................................

22. What is the conclusion of James' sentence, "Draw nigh to God—"? ...........................................................................

23. Who said of the temple, "Is it time for you, O ye, to dwell in your ceiled houses, and this house lie waste?"...........................

24. What is the other half of the couplet, "I will sing unto the Lord as long as I live"?.........................................................

............................................................................................

25. Who said, "Blessed is the man that trusteth in the Lord, and whose hope the Lord is"?....................................................

# BIBLE SAYINGS

## SERIES XV

1. What is Paul's saying about "our light affliction"?.....................

2. What is Christ's command urging us to be ready for his coming? ...........................................................................

3. Who wrote, "Cease ye from man, whose breath is in his nostrils"? ...............................................................................

4. Who said, "What evil thing is this that ye do, and profane the sabbath day?"..........................................................

5. Who said, "Be strong in the Lord, and in the power of his might"? ............................................................................

6. Who said, "With God all things are possible"?...........................

7. Of whom was it said that he was "a mighty hunter before the Lord"? ..........................................................................

8. Complete the couplet beginning, "The law of the Lord is perfect, converting the soul."................................................

9. To whom did the Lord say, "I have no pleasure in the death of the wicked"?...................................................................

10. Whose is the command, "Quench not the Spirit"?...................

11. Finish Christ's saying, "Let your light so shine before men—." ...........................................................................

12. What prophet said to Asa, "The Lord is with you, while ye be with him; and if ye seek him, he will be found of you; but if ye forsake him, he will forsake you"?...........................

13. To whom did God say, "Ye shall be unto me a kingdom of priests, and an holy nation"?................................................

14. What Book speaks of "the general assembly and church of the firstborn, which are written in heaven"?................................

15. To whom did Peter say, "Thy money perish with thee, because thou hast thought that the gift of God may be purchased with money"? .............................................................................

16. Who said, "There shall be one fold and one shepherd"?........
...........................................................................

17. Finish the proverb beginning, "My son, keep thy father's commandment—." ......................................................................................

18. Complete this verse from Job: "Happy is the man whom God correcteth: therefore—." ...........................................................

19. What is the rest of James' sentence, "Humble yourselves in the sight of the Lord, and—." ................................................

20. Who said, "Unto you is born this day in the city of David a Saviour, which is Christ the Lord"? To whom was it said?........
.................................................................................................................

21. Who uttered the prophecy, "I will also give thee for a light to the Gentiles, that thou mayest be my salvation unto the end of the earth"? ..............................................................................

22. What prophet said, "I will ransom them from the power of the grave; I will redeem them from death: O death, I will be thy plagues; O grave, I will be thy destruction"? ..........................

23. Who wrote: "Tribulation worketh patience; and patience, experience; and experience, hope"? ..............................................

24. Who warned against weeding the tares out from the wheat?

25. What Book says, "All the labor of man is for his mouth, and yet the appetite is not filled"? ...........................................................

## SERIES XVI

1. What did Christ say about his power over his own life?............

2. To whom did the Israelites say, "All that the Lord hath spoken we will do"? ....................................................................................

3. Complete the psalm couplet: "He shall deliver the needy when he crieth—." ......................................................................................

4. What did Paul say about "the wisdom of this world"?............
.................................................................................................................

5. Finish John's sentence, "If we say that we have no sin—."........
.................................................................................................................

6. "Before honor," says the proverb, is—what?...............................

7. Where was it said, "Go to, let us build us a city and a tower,

whose top may reach up to heaven"?.............................................

8. What prophet, describing women's attire, predicts for them "burning instead of beauty"?.............................................

9. What saying of Christ introduces dogs and pigs?...................

10. Whom did Paul advise, "Let no man despise thy youth"?........
.............................................................................................

11. To what church did Christ send the message, "Thou hast a little strength, and hast kept my word, and hast not denied my name"?.............................................

12. Finish the verse of the psalm: "Men shall be blessed in him—." .............................................

13. Where in the Bible is the reference to "the house of bondage"?

14. What is the prophecy in Daniel for those "that be wise"?........

15. Who said, "Many that are first shall be last; and the last first"? .............................................

16. Complete Paul's saying, "When we were yet without strength—." .............................................

17. Give the verse in Hebrews comparing the word of God to a sword. .............................................

18. Finish the verse, "Blessed are the undefiled in the way—."........

19. Who said, "When I bow down myself in the house of Rimmon, the Lord pardon thy servant in this thing"?...................

20. What is the saying about the bag with holes?...........................

21. Who said, "Unto whomsoever much is given, of him shall be much required"?.............................................

22. What is Paul's saying about the conflict between the flesh and the Spirit?.............................................

23. To whom did Elijah say, "The barrel of meal shall not waste, neither shall the cruise of oil fail, until the day that the Lord sendeth rain upon the earth"?.............................................

24. Who said, "Rebel not yet against the Lord, neither fear ye the people of the land; for they are bread for us"?...................

25. Who said of Christ, "He hath on his vesture and on his thigh a name written, KING OF KINGS AND LORD OF LORDS"?

# BIBLE SAYINGS

## SERIES XVII

1. Who said to the Israelites, "Thou shalt remember all the way which the Lord thy God led thee these forty years in the wilderness, to humble thee, and to prove thee"?..............................

2. Who sung, "Glory to God in the highest, and on earth peace, good will toward men"? Where?.....................................

3. Who wrote, "God commendeth his love toward us, in that, while we were yet sinners, Christ died for us"?...........................

4. Who upbraided David for his dancing before the Lord?............
   ..............................................................................................

5. What is the proverb about the power of the tongue?...............
   ..............................................................................................

6. What is Christ's saying about asking, seeking, and knocking?

7. Who said, "If ye had not plowed with my heifer, ye had not found out my riddle"?.............................................................

8. What is the psalmist's answer to the question, "Wherewithal shall a young man cleanse his way"?.......................................

9. What is the comparison of life to mist?.......................................

10. Who said, "As captain of the host of the Lord am I now come"? To whom did he speak?.................................................

11. Who prophesied, "They shall not hunger nor thirst; neither shall the heat nor sun smite them: for he that hath mercy on them shall lead them, even by the springs of water shall he guide them"?...............................................................................

12. Who said, "I have a baptism to be baptized with; and how am I straitened till it be accomplished!"?...........................................

13. What is the conclusion of Paul's exhortation, "Prove all things"? ...........................................................................................

14. What is the first Commandment?...............................................

15. What is the shuttle verse of Job?...............................................

16. What is the honeycomb comparison to God's judgments?........
    ..............................................................................................

17. Whom did Christ ask, "Can ye drink of the cup that I drink of? and be baptized with the baptism that I am baptized with"? ............................................................................................

18. What is Paul's saying urging thought about the unseen world?
............................................................................................

19. What is the verse in Revelation about the new heaven and new earth? ............................................................................................

20. What is the saying that begins, "Take with you words, and turn to the Lord—"?............................................................................................

21. Finish the sentence, "Thou shalt guide me with thy counsel—."
............................................................................................

22. Complete Isaiah's sentence, "He looked for judgment, but behold oppression;—."............................................................................................

23. What is the conclusion of Christ's saying, "If ye then, being evil, know how to give good gifts unto your children—"?........
............................................................................................

24. Complete Paul's sentence, "Whether Paul, or Apollos, or Cephas, or the world, or life, or death, or things present, or things to come,—."............................................................................................

25. Who said, "I perceive that thou art in the gall of bitterness, and in the bond of iniquity"? To whom was he speaking?

## SERIES XVIII

1. What is the saying in Ecclesiastes about the house of mourning? ............................................................................................

2. To whom did God say, "I will bless thee, and thou shalt be a blessing"? ............................................................................................

3. What did Christ say about his sheep?............................................................................................

4. Whom did Paul urge, "Neglect not the gift that is in thee"?

5. Finish the sentence, "Thy word have I hid in mine heart—."

6. What is the second Commandment?............................................................................................

7. In what Book are the words, "Thou shalt remember the Lord thy God: for it is he that giveth thee power to get wealth"?

# BIBLE SAYINGS

8. Finish the proverb, "Can a man take fire in his bosom—."..........

9. What parable ends with the words, "Then shall the righteous shine forth as the sun in the kingdom of their Father"?............

10. Complete Paul's saying, "As by one man's disobedience many were made sinners—.".....................

11. Finish James's sentence, "To him that knoweth to do good, and doeth it not—." ....................

12. Who said, "Lord, now lettest thou thy servant depart in peace?" On what occasion?......................

13. What is Jeremiah's saying about the deceitful heart?...............

14. Who said, "Hear now, ye rebels; must we fetch you water out of this rock?" Where?......................

15. What is the chief proverb about friendship?....................

16. What did Christ say about the fulfilment of Scripture?............

17. What is "the fruit of the Spirit?".....................

18. What is the prophecy of "the desire of all nations"?...............

19. What is Paul's list of the gospel armor?......................

20. What is Ezekiel's saying about the stony heart?......................

21. Who said, "I would not live alway"?......................

22. Complete the verse of the psalm, "He satisfieth the longing soul—." .....................

23. Who said, "With the jawbone of an ass, heaps upon heaps, with the jawbone of an ass have I slain a thousand men"?

24. Where is it said of Christ that he was "in all points tempted like as we are, yet without sin"?......................

25. To what church did Christ say, "Because thou art lukewarm. and neither cold nor hot, I will spue thee out of my mouth"?

# BIBLE SAYINGS

## SERIES XIX

1. What is the first verse of John's Gospel?.....................................
2. What prophet speaks about "making the ephah small, and the shekel great, and falsifying the balances by deceit"?..........

3. Who said, "Art thou he that troubleth Israel?" To whom did he say it?.....................................................................................
4. Finish this sentence from I John: "If we confess our sins—."

5. What prophet said, "The eyes of the Lord run to and fro throughout the whole earth, to show himself strong in the behalf of them whose heart is perfect toward him"?....................
6. Who said, "Shout; for the Lord hath given you the city"? To what city did he refer?............................................................
7. What Book says, "Our God is a consuming fire"?...................
8. Who said, "My kingdom is not of this world"?.......................,
9. Who said, "The leprosy therefore of Naaman shall cleave unto thee, and to thy seed forever"? To whom was he speaking? ...........................................................................................................
10. Who said, "Behold, this dreamer cometh"? To whom did they refer? ....................................................................................................
11. Repeat the prayer beginning, "Let the words of my mouth—."

12. Who said, "Except ye repent, ye shall all likewise perish"?
13. Who said "To me to live is Christ, and to die is gain"?...........
14. In what Book is the promise regarding the hereafter, "God shall wipe away all tears from their eyes"?...............................
15. Who asked, "How shall a man be just with God?"...................
16. What is the third Commandment? ..............................................

17. Who said, "I set before you this day a blessing and a curse"?
18. Who said, "Woe unto them that are wise in their own eyes, and prudent in their own sight!"?...........................................

# BIBLE SAYINGS

19. What is Christ's saying about the right eye offending?............

20. What is Paul's saying about being dead to sin?............

21. What proverb tells us what to do with God's commandments?

22. Finish the verse, "My flesh and my heart faileth: but—."............

23. Complete Christ's saying, "The Son of man came not to be ministered unto—."............

24. In whose prophecy is God's promise, "I will heal their backsliding, I will love them freely"?............

25. Finish the prayer of the psalm: "Open thou mine eyes that—."

## SERIES XX

1. Who said, "Swear not at all"?............

2. Who said, "If any provide not for his own, and specially for those of his own house, he hath denied the faith, and is worse than an infidel"?............

3. Of whom was it said, "A sword shall pierce through thy own soul also"? Who said it?............

4. Who wrote, "In the name of our God we will set up our banners"?

5. Who said generously, "Is not the whole land before thee?" To whom did he say it?............

6. Of whom did Jehoshaphat say, "I hate him; for he never prophesied good unto me, but always evil"?............

7. Who wrote, "Heal me, O Lord, and I shall be healed; save me, and I shall be saved"?............

8. What did Christ say was the reason for his coming into the world?

## BIBLE SAYINGS

9. Complete Paul's prophecy: "We know that if our earthly house of this tabernacle were dissolved—."................................

............................................................................................................

10. Of whose vision was it said, "Everything shall live whither the river cometh"?..............................................................

11. What is the fourth Commandment?................................................

12. Finish the proverb, "He that hath pity upon the poor—."...........

............................................................................................................

13. Who compared the kingdom of heaven to a "pearl of great price"? .................................................................................

14. What is Paul's statement about the requirement of a steward? .............................................................................

15. What is Christ's saying about the narrow gate?........................

............................................................................................................

16. To what does Ecclesiastes compare the laughter of fools?........

............................................................................................................

17. What prophet predicted a famine, "not a famine of bread, nor a thirst for water, but of hearing the words of the Lord"?

18 What Book tells of those "that go down to the sea in ships, that do business in great waters"?.............................................

19. Who were made "hewers of wood and drawers of water," and why? .......................................................................................

20. Who said, "The Lord God hath given me the tongue of the learned, that I should know how to speak a word in season to him that is weary"?............................................................

21. What is Christ's affirmation of union with God?........................

............................................................................................................

22. What is the promise in the Revelation to him "that overcometh"? ...............................................................................

23. What is the psalmist's expression of delight in God's law?........

............................................................................................................

24. Who said, "Let me die with the Philistines"?............................

25. Who said, "Understandest thou what thou readest?" and to whom was he speaking?......................................................

# BIBLE SAYINGS

## SERIES XXI

1.  Who said, "Fear not: for they that be with us are more than they that be with them"? On what occasion?..............................
2.  Who said, "The silver is mine, and the gold is mine, saith the Lord of hosts"?..............................................................
3.  Who called Herod "That fox"?.............................................
4.  What are Paul's two commands about burden-bearing?............
.......................................................................................
5.  What is the Golden Rule?...................................................
6.  In what Book are the questions, "Canst thou by searching find out God? Canst thou find out the Almighty unto perfection?"
.......................................................................................
7.  Who asked, "How long halt ye between two opinions? if the Lord be God, follow him: but if Baal, then follow him"?..........
8.  Who said, "Our soul loatheth this light bread"?......................
9.  Who commanded, "Abstain from all appearance of evil"?......
10. Where in the Bible is the benediction beginning, "The Lord hear thee in the day of trouble"?..............................................
11. Finish the sentence, "Let us therefore come boldly unto the throne of grace—."...............................................................
12. Who said, "How can I do this great wickedness, and sin against God?" To whom was he speaking?..............................
13. What is the fifth Commandment?...........................................
14. Who said, "Behold, we count them happy which endure"?
15. Where did Christ say, "A prophet is not without honor, save in his own country, and in his own house"?..............................
16. What prophet wrote: "Though thou exalt thyself as the eagle, and though thou set thy nest among the stars, thence will I bring thee down, saith the Lord"?..............................................
17. What verse of the psalms compares the Bible to a lantern?
18. Complete this verse of Isaiah: "Therefore the redeemed of the Lord shall return, and come with singing unto Zion; and everlasting joy shall be upon their head—."................................

37

19. In what Book is the prophecy: "The Lord thy God will raise up unto thee a prophet from the midst of thee, of thy brethren, like unto me; unto him ye shall harken"?...........................

20. What king said to his judges, "Deal courageously, and the Lord shall be with the good"?...........................................

21. What is the proverb comparing wisdom to rubies?...................
...................................................................................................

22. Who said, "Behold the man!" Of whom did he say it?............
...................................................................................................

23. Who said, "It is hard for thee to kick against the pricks"? To whom did he say it?........................................................

24. Finish the verse, "Thy way, O God, is in the sanctuary—."
...................................................................................................

25. What prophet said, "Cursed be the day wherein I was born"?

## SERIES XXII

1. Through what prophet did God say, "I am like a green fir tree. From me is thy fruit found"?........................................

2. Who said, "If I do not the works of my Father, believe me not"? ...........................................................................

3. Finish Paul's saying, "Let nothing be done through strife or vainglory—." ...................................................................

4. To whom did God say, "All the land which thou seest, to thee will I give it, and to thy seed forever"?...............................

5. What does the psalmist say is "the beginning of wisdom"?
...................................................................................................

6. What prophet saw trees, "the fruit thereof shall be for meat, and the leaf thereof for medicine"?......................................

7. What is the conclusion of Christ's saying, "Let your communication be Yea, yea; Nay, nay: for—"?...................................

8. Who said to Christ, "Lord, what wilt thou have me to do"?........

9. Complete the saying regarding Christ, "Though he were a Son,—." ...................................................................................

10. What is Isaiah's condemnation of great land holdings?............

11. Who said, "Sun, stand thou still upon Gibeon; and thou, Moon, in the valley of Ajalon"?.................................................

12. What is the sixth Commandment?.................................................

13. What psalm verse begins, "The entrance of thy words giveth light"? .................................................

14. Who cried, "Jesus, thou Son of David, have mercy on me"?

15. What saying of Paul's urges the payment of pastors' salaries?

16. What is the saying in Ecclesiastes teaching us not to over-rate the past?.................................................

17. Who said, "The Lord deal kindly with you, as ye have dealt with the dead, and with me"? To whom did she say it?...........

18. What verse in John describes Christ's work in creation?.........

19. To whom did Abraham say, "I will not take anything that is thine, lest thou shouldest say, I have made Abram rich"?........

20. Who said, "How shall I curse, whom God hath not cursed? or how shall I defy, whom the Lord hath not defied?".............

21. In what prophecy are the words, "Rend your heart, and not your garments, and turn unto the Lord your God: for he is gracious and merciful, slow to anger, and of great kindness, and repenteth him of the evil"?.................................................

22. Finish Paul's saying, "If thou shalt confess with thy mouth the Lord Jesus—."..............................................

23. What is the conclusion of the verse, "I saw no temple therein—"? .................................................

24. Who said, "Do not interpretations belong to God?"...............

25. Who said, "It is not lawful for thee to have her?" To whom and concerning whom did he speak?.................................................

# BIBLE SAYINGS

## SERIES XXIII

1. Who said, "Give alms of such things as ye have"?....................
2. Who wrote, "Walk worthy of God, who hath called you unto his kingdom and glory"? In what Book?......................
3. In what Book are the words, "Before they call, I will answer; and while they are yet speaking, I will hear"?............................
4. Who named a stone Eben-ezer, meaning, "Hitherto hath the Lord helped us"?............................
5. Who wrote, "The fool hath said in his heart, There is no God"?
6. Who said of God, "His kingdom is an everlasting kingdom"? ............................
7. Who said, "We cannot but speak the things which we have seen and heard"? In what Book?............................
8. Who wrote, "The kingdoms of this world are become the kingdoms of our Lord, and of his Christ; and he shall reign for ever and ever"? In what Book?............................
9. Who said, "All things are possible to him that believeth"? To whom did he say it?............................
10. Who said, "Let there be light," and there was light? In what Book? ............................
11. In what Book is the benediction, "The Lord bless thee, and keep thee: the Lord make his face shine upon thee, and be gracious unto thee: the Lord lift up his countenance upon thee, and give thee peace"?............................
12. Who said, "He that is not with me is against me"?....................
13. Who wrote, "Walk in love"?............................
14. Who wrote, "The tongue is a fire"?............................
15. In what Book is the expression, "The valley of Achor for a door of hope"?............................
16. Who said, "I am but a little child: I know not how to go out or come in"?............................
17. Who said, "Choose you this day whom ye will serve"?............
18. Who said, "We have seen his star in the east"?....................

# BIBLE SAYINGS

19. Who wrote, "I am not ashamed of the gospel of Christ"? In what Book?....................................................................................

20. In what Book is the question, "How shall we escape, if we neglect so great salvation?"..................................................

21. Who wrote, "A bruised reed shall he not break, and smoking flax shall he not quench"?...............................................

22. In what Book is this found: "Every beast of the forest is mine, and the cattle upon a thousand hills"?...........................

23. Who said, "My father, my father, the chariot of Israel, and the horsemen thereof"? Of whom did he say it?......................

24. Who said, "The Lord gave, and the Lord hath taken away; blessed be the name of the Lord"?.....................................

25. To whom was it said, "I have made thee a watchman unto the house of Israel"?..............................................................

## SERIES XXIV

1. Who said, "Ye shall know the truth, and the truth shall make you free"?.......................................................................

2. Who wrote, "God hath chosen the weak things of the world to confound the things which are mighty"?............................

3. Who said, "This day shall be unto you for a memorial"? Through whom did he say it, and of what day?.........................
   ....................................................................................

4. Who said, "The fear of the Lord, that is wisdom; and to depart from evil is understanding"?......................................

5. Who said, "Go ye into all the world, and preach the gospel to every creature"?..........................................................

6. In what Book is the description of a woman, that she is "fair as the moon, clear as the sun, and terrible as an army with banners"? ....................................................................

7. Who wrote, "I am crucified with Christ"?..............................

8. Who prayed, "Oh that I had wings like a dove! for then would I fly away, and be at rest"?.........................................

9. Who said, "Thou wilt cast all their sins into the depths of the sea"? ....................................................................................................

10. Who wrote, "Christ came into the world to save sinners, of whom I am chief"?....................................................................................

11. Who said, "How are the mighty fallen!" On what occasion?

12. In what Book is the saying, "Ye that love the Lord, hate evil"? ....................................................................................................

13. In what Book do we find: "Whatsoever God doeth, it shall be for ever"?....................................................................................

14. Who wrote, "All the promises of God in him [Christ] are yea, and in him Amen"?....................................................................................

15. In what Book is the sentence, "The eyes of the Lord are in every place, beholding the evil and the good"?................................... ....................................................................................................

16. Whose preaching is summed up in the words, "Repent ye: for the kingdom of heaven is at hand"?...................................................

17. Who wrote, "Unto the pure all things are pure"?...........................

18. Who said, "Ye shall not fear them, for the Lord your God he shall fight for you"? To whom did he say it?........................

19. In what Book is the exhortation, "Let everything that hath breath praise the Lord"?....................................................................

20. Of whom was it said that "he endured, as seeing him who is invisible"? In what Book is the saying?...........................................

21. In what Book is it commanded, "Put difference between holy and unholy, and between unclean and clean"?.............................

22. Who said, "Shall I drink the blood of these men, that have put their lives in jeopardy?" and on what occasion?...................

23. Who wrote, "No prophecy of the scripture is of any private interpretation"? ....................................................................................

24. Of whom was it said that he "had prepared his heart to seek the law of the Lord, and to do it, and to teach in Israel statutes and judgments"? ....................................................................

25. Who wrote the benediction beginning, "Now unto him that is able to keep you from falling"?....................................................

# BIBLE SAYINGS

## SERIES XXV

1. Who enacted the law "that every man should bear rule in his own house"?..................................................................

2. Who said, "As thy days, so shall thy strength be"? Of whom was it said?...............................................................

3. Who said, "The fear of the Lord is the beginning of knowledge? ...................................................................

4. Who said, "Out of the abundance of the heart the mouth speaketh"? ...................................................................

5. Who wrote, "Study to be quiet, and to do your own business, and to work with your own hands"? To whom was he writing? ...........................................................

6. Who said, "All that a man hath will he give for his life"? Of whom did he say it?.............................................

7. Who said, "Let us make man in our image, after our likeness"? ...................................................................

8. Who wrote, "Make a joyful noise unto the Lord, all the earth"? ...................................................................

9. Who said, "Ah, Lord God! behold, I cannot speak: for I am a child"? On what occasion?.........................................

10. Who said, "Lord, I believe; help thou mine unbelief"? To whom did he say it?.............................................

11. In what Book is it said of the Christians, "They loved not their lives unto the death"?.........................................

12. Who said, "My people are destroyed for lack of knowledge"? ...................................................................

13. Who wrote, "The just shall live by his faith"?.........................

14. Who said, "Thou hast not lied unto men, but unto God"? To whom did he say it?.............................................

15. In what Book is the saying, "A wise son maketh a glad father"? ...................................................................

16. Who said, "Fear ye not, stand still, and see the salvation of the Lord"? To whom was he speaking? On what occasion?

.....................................................................................................

17. Who said, "The Lord thy God is a consuming fire"?...............

.....................................................................................................

18. Who said, "Blessed art thou among women"? To whom was it said? ...........................................................................................

19. Who wrote, "Our sufficiency is of God"?.....................................

.....................................................................................................

20. Who wrote, "So built we the wall; for the people had a mind to work"? ..................................................................................

21. Who wrote, "Cast thy burden upon the Lord, and he shall sustain thee"?...............................................................................

22. Who said, "Even the very hairs of your head are all numbered"? ...............................................................................

23. In what Book is the saying, "Ye shall keep my sabbaths, and reverence my sanctuary"?.........................................................

24. Who offered the prayer, "Hear thou in heaven thy dwelling place: and when thou hearest, forgive"?....................................

.....................................................................................................

25. Who said, "Bring forth therefore fruits meet for repentance"?

## SERIES XXVI

1. Who wrote, "Unto him that loved us, and washed us from our sins in his own blood, and hath made us kings and priests unto God and his Father; to him be glory and dominion for ever and ever"? In what Book?.....................................................

2. Who wrote about "the chambers of imagery"?............................

3. Who said of the devil, "He is a liar, and the father of it"?........

.....................................................................................................

4. Who prayed, "Wash me, and I shall be whiter than snow"?

5. Who said, "Thy love to me was wonderful, passing the love of women"? Of whom did he say it?...........................................

6.  In what Book is the saying, "A threefold cord is not quickly broken"? .........................................................................

7.  Who wrote, "I determined not to know anything among you, save Jesus Christ, and him crucified"? To whom was he writing? ......................

8.  Who wrote, "The lines are fallen unto me in pleasant places: yea, I have a goodly heritage"?...................................................

9.  Who said, "It is not good that man should be alone"?...............

10. Who said, "The stars in their courses fought against Sisera"?

11. Who wrote, "Wherein thou judgest another, thou condemnest thyself"? .........................................................................

12. Who said, "Go up, thou bald head; go up, thou bald head," and to whom?...............................................................

13. In what Book does God say, "When thou passest through the waters, I will be with thee"?...........................................

14. In what Book is the saying, "The Lord is good, a strong hold in the day of trouble; and he knoweth them that trust in him"? .........................................................................

15. Who wrote, "Awake thou that sleepest, and arise from the dead, and Christ shall give thee light"? In what Book?............
.........................................................................

16. Who said, "The Spirit of the Lord will come upon thee, and thou shalt be turned into another man"? To whom did he say it? .........................................................................

17. Who was it who denied that he had eaten his morsel alone?
.........................................................................

18. In what Book is it said, "Love is strong as death; jealousy is cruel as the grave"?...........................................

19. Who said, "If a man keep my saying, he shall never see death"? .........................................................................

20. In what Book is the benediction, "Now unto the King eternal, immortal, invisible, the only wise God, be honor and glory for ever and ever. Amen"?...........................................
.........................................................................

21. Who wrote, "The Lord knoweth how to deliver the godly out of temptations"?....................................................................................

22. Where is the sentence, "Wherefore seeing we also are compassed about with so great a cloud of witnesses, let us lay aside every weight, and the sin which doth so easily beset us, and let us run with patience the race that is set before us, looking unto Jesus the author and finisher of our faith; who for the joy that was set before him endured the cross, despising the shame, and is set down at the right hand of the throne of God"?....................................................................................

23. Who said, "The eternal God is thy refuge, and underneath are the everlasting arms"?....................................................................................

24. Who said, "Who knoweth whether thou art come to the kingdom for such a time as this"? and to whom was it said?

....................................................................................

25. Who said, "We ought to obey God rather than men"?................

# BIBLE SAYINGS

## SERIES XXVII

1. Who said, "Wist ye not that I must be about my Father's business"? On what occasion?......................................................

2. Who wrote, "The kingdom of God is not in word, but in power"? ..........................................................................................

3. Who wrote of the heavenly city, "The glory of God did lighten it, and the Lamb is the light thereof"?.......................................

4. What is the proverb describing wine as a mocker?...................
......................................................................................................

5. Who said, "We do not well: this day is a day of good tidings, and we hold our peace"?..................................................................

6. Who said, "The Lord hath need of him"? Concerning what?

7. What is Paul's saying about the wages of sin?..........................
......................................................................................................

8. Who wrote, "The prayer of faith shall save the sick"?...............
......................................................................................................

9. What is the verse of the psalm about trusting in chariots?........
......................................................................................................

10. Who said, "I will call upon the Lord, and he shall send thunder and rain"?................................................................................

11. Who said to his advisers, "No doubt but ye are the people, and wisdom shall die with you"?...................................................

12. Who wrote, "Whilst we are at home in the body, we are absent from the Lord"?...........................................................................

13. What ruler asked of Jesus, "What is truth"?.............................

14. In what Book is the prophecy, "I will bring forth my servant the Branch"?.....................................................................................

15. Who asked his followers to pray for him, "that the word of the Lord may have free course, and be glorified"?.....................

16. On what occasion did the people cry, "The Lord, he is the God; the Lord, he is the God"?.................................................

17. What psalm verse did Christ quote on the cross?...................

18. What saying of Christ's introduces a hen and her chickens?
.............................................................................................................

19. What is Paul's saying about godliness and contentment?...
.............................................................................................................

20. Quote Christ's saying about figs and thistles.............................
21. What is Paul's saying about calling on Christ's name?............
.............................................................................................................

22. Who said, "The Father is in me, and I in him"?.......................
23. Quote Paul's hymn of Christian love............................................
.............................................................................................................

24. Who said, "Be of good courage, and let us play the men for
    our people, and for the cities of our God: and the Lord do
    that which seemeth him good"?.................................................

25. In what Book is this account of the heavenly city: "There
    shall in no wise enter into it anything that defileth, neither
    whatsoever worketh abomination, or maketh a lie: but they
    which are written in the Lamb's book of life"?...........................

## SERIES XXVIII

1. Quote the advice regarding prosperity and adversity given in
   Ecclesiastes. ......................................................................................

2. Who prophesied, "There shall come a Star out of Jacob, and
   a Sceptre shall rise out of Israel"?.................................................

3. Who said, "Though he slay me, yet will I trust him"?...................

4. Complete John's saying, "In him was life—."...............................

5. Who advised, "Let all things be done decently and in order"?
   .............................................................................................................

6. To whom was it said, and about whom, "He is a chosen vessel
   unto me, to bear my name before the Gentiles"?.......................

7. To what prophet was it said, "I will pour out my spirit upon
   all flesh; and your sons and your daughters shall prophesy,
   your old men shall dream dreams, your young men shall see
   visions"? .............................................................................................

# BIBLE SAYINGS

8. In what Book is it said, "So we thy people and sheep of thy pasture will give thee thanks forever"? ......................................

9. What is the seventh Commandment?..............................................
......................................................................................................

10. Who cried, "Holy, holy, holy, is the Lord of hosts: the whole earth is full of his glory"?..................................................

11. Who sung, "Hosanna; blessed is he that cometh in the name of the Lord"? On what occasion?..................................................

12. Finish Paul's saying, "A little leaven—."..................................

13. Who said, "What I have written, I have written"? In what connection? ..........................................................................

14. Who said, "Here am I; send me"? When?..................................

15. To whom did God say, "Is anything too hard for the Lord"? In what connection?..................................................................

16. Repeat Ruth's declaration that she would go with Naomi.........
......................................................................................................

17. What did Christ say about turning the other cheek?....................
......................................................................................................

18. What is the verse about entertaining angels?..............................
......................................................................................................

19. How did Paul describe the struggle between what he loved and what he hated?..................................................................

20. How did Christ sum up his instructions about seeking the best seats at a feast?..................................................................

21. To whom was it said, "What meanest thou, O sleeper"? On what occasion? ..........................................................................

22. What is the conclusion of the verse, "From the rising of the sun unto the going down of the same—."..................................

23. Finish Paul's sentence, "The Lord direct your hearts into the love of God—."................................................................

24. Of whom did Christ say, "This sickness is not unto death, but for the glory of God"?..................................................

25. What is the proverb about "divers weights and measures"?....
......................................................................................................

# BIBLE SAYINGS

## SERIES XXIX

1.   What is the proverb about "even a child"?.................................

2.   Who said, "By their fruits ye shall know them"?....................
3.   Who said, "Tabitha, arise"?..........................................
4.   Who said, "I do remember my faults this day"?  On what occasion? ........................................................................
5.   Where is the saying, "Thine eye shall not pity, but life shall go for life, eye for eye, tooth for tooth, hand for hand, foot for foot"? ..............................................................
6.   Who said, "Behold, there ariseth a little cloud out of the sea, like a man's hand"?  On what occasion?..............................
7.   Who said, "They need not depart; give ye them to eat"?........

8.   Who said, "As many as I love, I rebuke and chasten: be zealous therefore, and repent"?  In what Book?............................
9.   What were Paul's orders about labor?.....................................

10.  Where is the saying, "Great peace have they which love thy law"? ........................................................................
11.  What is the eighth Commandment?............................................

12.  Who said, "Is thy servant a dog, that he should do this great thing"? ....................................................................
13.  Repeat Ps. 23. ...............................................................

14.  Where is the sentence, "I am the rose of Sharon, and the lily of the valleys"?...........................................................
15.  Who said, "The wedding is ready, but they which were bidden were not worthy"?.................................................
16.  Who asked, "How shall they hear without a preacher?"..........

## BIBLE SAYINGS

17. Where is the saying, "He that is unjust, let him be unjust still"? .....................................................................................

18. Who said, "One man of you shall chase a thousand: for the Lord your God, he it is that fighteth for you, as he hath promised you"? .........................................................................

19. Who said, "How beautiful upon the mountains are the feet of him that bringeth good tidings, that publisheth peace"?..........
...................................................................................................

20. Finish the proverb concerning wisdom, "I love them that love me—."................................................................................

21. Who wrote, "We walk by faith, not by sight"?.........................

22. Who said, "O generation of vipers, who hath warned you to flee from the wrath to come?".................................................

23. Finish Paul's saying, "Be not deceived; God is not mocked—."
...................................................................................................

24. Who spoke the parable about the poor man's little ewe lamb?
...................................................................................................

25. When did Christ say, "Woman, behold thy son!" To whom was he speaking, and with reference to whom?.......................
...................................................................................................

## SERIES XXX

1. Where is the prophecy, "In that day shall ye call every man his neighbor under the vine and under the fig tree"?...............

2. Who said, "It may be that the Lord will work for us: for there is no restraint to the Lord to save by many or by few"?..........

3. What prophet reported these words from the Lord, "Ye shall seek me, and find me, when ye shall search for me with all your heart"?....................................................................................

4. Finish Paul's saying, "Look not every man on his own things—." .........................................................................................

5. Who said, "My house shall be called of all nations the house of prayer, but ye have made it a den of thieves"?.......................

51

6. In what Book is the prophecy, "Behold, a virgin shall conceive, and bear a son, and shall call his name Immanuel"?......

7. Of whom is it said that he "became mighty, because he prepared his ways before the Lord his God"?.....................

8. Who said, "The love of money is the root of all evil"?............

9. What is the ninth Commandment?...............................................

10. Who said, "Man that is born of a woman is of few days and full of trouble"?......................................................................

11. What is the first part of the saying which ends, "Let us go on unto perfection"? .............................................................

12. What is the saying about "effectual fervent prayer"?.............

13. What is Christ's saying about "the highways and hedges"?.....

14. Who said, "Thou art the man"? And to whom did he say it?

15. Finish the verse of the psalm which begins, "The earth is the Lord's." .................................................................................

16. Who said, "All thy billows and thy waves passed over me"?....
................................................................................................

17. Who wrote, "Christ our passover is sacrificed for us"?..............

18. Finish John's saying, "The law was given by Moses, but—."

19. Who said to the Israelites, "Ye have compassed this mountain long enough"? .......................................................................

20. Who asked, "Friend, how camest thou in hither not having a wedding garment"?....................................................................

21. To whom did the Lord say, "What God hath cleansed, that call not thou common"?.......................................................................

22. What prophet cried, "Multitudes, multitudes, in the valley of decision: for the day of the Lord is near in the valley of decision"? ...............................................................................

23. Who said, "It is not in me: God shall give Pharaoh an answer of peace"? ..............................................................................

24. Who said, "To obey is better than sacrifice," and to whom did he say it?..................................................................................

25. Who said, "We have toiled all the night, and have taken nothing: nevertheless at thy word I will let down the net"?..............

# BIBLE SAYINGS

## SERIES XXXI

1. Who said, "This day I am going the way of all the earth"?........

2. What is the proverb about bargaining?.........................................

3. What prophet wrote, "Not by might, nor by power, but by my spirit, saith the Lord of hosts"?......................

4. What is Christ's saying about the second mile?........................

5. Of whom was it said, "These that have turned the world upside down are come hither also"?......................

6. Who wrote, "Let this mind be in you, which was also in Christ Jesus"?......................

7. Who asked, "If a man die, shall he live again"? and what did he add?......................

8. What is the tenth Commandment?......................

9. Of whom was it said, "He driveth furiously"?......................

10. What is the first part of the sentence, ending, "from whence cometh my help"?......................

11. Finish Isaiah's sentence, "The people that walked in darkness—." ......................

12. Who said, "Touch me not," and to whom did he say it?...............

13. Whom did Paul exhort, "Fight the good fight of faith"?...........

14. Finish the verse in the Revelation, "Behold, I stand at the door, and knock"?......................

15. To whom did the Lord say, "I have loved thee with an everlasting love"?......................

16. What is the conclusion of Christ's sentence, "Not every one that saith unto me, Lord, Lord, shall enter into the kingdom of heaven—"?......................

17. What does James say about the rewards for converting sinners? ......................

18. How does Amos describe the oppressions of the rich?..............

19. Who said, "Shall not the Judge of all the earth do right"? On what occasion?................

20. Who said, "God hath made man upright; but they have sought out many inventions"?................

21. Who said, "Be of good cheer; it is I; be not afraid"? On what occasion? ................

22. Who cried, "O wretched man that I am! who shall deliver me from the body of this death?"................

23. Who wrote of Christ, "Whom having not seen, ye love; in whom, though now ye see him not, yet believing, ye rejoice with joy unspeakable and full of glory"?................

24. Finish the verse of the psalm beginning, "I love the Lord, because—." ................

25. In what Book is the verse, "He brought me to the banqueting house, and his banner over me was love"?................

## SERIES XXXII

1. Complete Christ's saying, "What things soever ye desire, when ye pray—."................

2. What is Paul's sentence linking together "faith" and "hearing"? ................

3. What is the invitation verse of the Revelation?................

4. Who said, "With him is an arm of flesh, but with us is the Lord our God to help us, and to fight our battles." Of what enemy was he speaking?................

5. What is the proverb about sinning against wisdom?................

6. Who said, "Many are called, but few are chosen"?................

# BIBLE SAYINGS

7. Who wrote, "Christ died for our sins according to the scriptures"? ....................................................................................

8. Finish the statement in Hebrews, that Christ was made, "not after the law of a carnal commandment, but—.".........................
.....................................................................................................

9. What is the psalm verse about "the finest of the wheat"?........
.....................................................................................................

10. Who said, "Behold the Lamb of God, which taketh away the sin of the world"?...........................................................................

11. Who wrote, "The love of God constraineth us"?......................

12. What is the last verse of the Bible?...........................................

13. What does Deuteronomy say about paying vows?.....................
.....................................................................................................

14. Finish the psalm verse beginning, "Justice and judgment are the habitation of thy throne—.".................................................

15. What does Paul say about being weary in well doing?............
.....................................................................................................

16. To whom did Christ say, "I am the resurrection and the life"?
.....................................................................................................

17. What metaphor does Paul use regarding baptism?....................
.....................................................................................................

18. How does the psalmist express his longing for God's house?
.....................................................................................................

19. Who wrote, "Be not weary in well doing"?...............................

20. What prophet asks, "Can two walk together, except they be agreed"? .......................................................................................

21. Where is it said, "Marriage is honorable in all"?......................

22. Who said, "This city is near to flee unto, and it is a little one: Oh, let me escape thither, (is it not a little one?) and my soul shall live"?...............................................................................

23. What did Christ say about hating one's own family?...............
.....................................................................................................

24. What is Paul's "no condemnation" verse?.................................

25. What did Christ say about lending?...........................................

## SERIES XXXIII

1. Who asked, "Can we find such a one as this is, a man in whom the Spirit of God is"?.....................

2. Who said, "Thou hast rejected the word of the Lord, and the Lord hath rejected thee from being king over Israel"? To whom was he speaking?.....................

3. What was Christ's answer when the leper said, "Lord, if thou wilt, thou canst make me clean"?.....................

4. In what Book did the expression, "Touch not; taste not; handle not," originate?.....................

5. Who wrote, "The gifts and calling of God are without repentance"? .....................

6. On what great occasion did Christ say, "Peace be unto you"?

7. Finish Isaiah's sentence, "They shall see eye to eye—."...........

8. Who said, "Fear not: for God is come to prove you, and that his fear may be before your faces, that ye sin not"? When?....
   ..................................................................

9. Complete the verse of the psalm, "Blessed is the people that know the joyful sound—."....................

10. Who cried, "Yet forty days, and Nineveh shall be overthrown"? .....................

11. Who said to Christ, "Depart from me, for I am a sinful man, O Lord"? When?.....................

12. Finish Paul's sentence, "As we have therefore opportunity—."

13. Who said, "Miserable comforters are ye all"? To whom?........

14. In what Book is the command, "Thou shalt not muzzle the ox when he treadeth out the corn"?.....................

15. What verse in Isaiah contains five titles of Christ?.....................

16. What was Christ's decision in regard to paying taxes to the Romans? .....................

17. Who said, "Stand up; I myself also am a man"? On what occasion? .....................

# BIBLE SAYINGS

18. What is Paul's advice to the rich?......................................................
19. To whom did Christ say, "O thou of little faith, wherefore didst thou doubt"? On what occasion?........................................
20. What prophet asked, "Who hath despised the day of small things"? ................................................................................
21. When was it said of Manasseh that he "knew that the Lord he was God"?....................................................................
22. Finish the psalm verse: "The Lord is thy keeper—."..................
...............................................................................................................
23. Who said, "God hath made me to laugh, so that all that hear will laugh with me"? On what occasion?....................................
24. Who wrote, "I will put my law in their inward parts, and write it in their hearts"?................................................................
25. What did Christ say about marriage in heaven?...........................

## SERIES XXXIV

1. Who said, "We have found the Messias"?....................................
2. Finish the song of the angels beginning, "Worthy is the Lamb that was slain—."............................................................................
3. What is the answer to the psalmist's question, "Who shall ascend into the hill of the Lord? or who shall stand in his holy place?" ................................................................................
4. Who said, "I shall go to him, but he shall not return to me"? On what occasion?....................................................................
5. What is the description of spring in Solomon's Song?.................
6. Who said, "By the grace of God I am what I am"?......................
7. Who shouted, "Lazarus, come forth!" When?.............................
8. Who said of Christ, "He is the propitiation for our sins: and not for ours only, but also for the sins of the whole world"?
...............................................................................................................
9. Who said, "Come with me, and see my zeal for the Lord"? To whom did he say it?....................................................................
10. What is Christ's command to love enemies?.............................

# BIBLE SAYINGS

11. Who said, "Gird up the loins of your mind, be sober"?............
12. Of whom is it said that they "received the word with all readiness of mind, and searched the scriptures daily, whether those things were so"?......................................................................
13. In what Book is the sentence, "There is no discharge in that war"? .........................................................................................
14. What did the psalmist say in his haste?......................................
15. What is Paul's saying about being bought with a price?............
    ....................................................................................................
16. Complete the proverb, "Love not sleep—."................................
    ....................................................................................................
17. What did Christ say about titles?................................................
18. What did Paul say about the newness of the Christian life?....
    ....................................................................................................
19. What does the psalmist say about those that trust in the Lord?
    ....................................................................................................
20. What reason for contentment is given in Hebrews?..................
    ....................................................................................................
21. What does the proverb say is "the beginning of wisdom"?........
    ....................................................................................................
22. What is Paul's saying about working out one's salvation?........
    ....................................................................................................
23. What is the prophecy about children playing in the streets?
24. Who said, "I cast it [the gold] into the fire, and there came out this calf"?..............................................................................
25. Who said, "The Strength of Israel will not lie nor repent: for he is not a man, that he should repent"?......................................

# BIBLE SAYINGS

## SERIES XXXV

1. What verse describes God's impartiality?......................................
2. What did Christ say about "times" and "seasons"?.....................
3. What is Zechariah's prophecy of Christ's atonement?.................
4. What Book speaks of the little foxes that spoil the vines?...........
..............................................................................................................
5. Who said, "The Lord watch between me and thee, when we are absent one from another"? To whom was he speaking?............
..............................................................................................................
6. Who said, "The foxes have holes, and the birds of the air have nests," but he had not "where to lay his head"?..........................
7. Who said, "I AM THAT I AM"? To whom did he tell this name?
8. What does James say about enduring temptation?.....................
..............................................................................................................
9. What proverb advises good counsel?............................................
10. Who said, "The battle is the Lord's, and he will give you into our hands"? To whom did he say it?...............................................
11. What did Christ say about the hairs of our head?.......................
..............................................................................................................
12. What expression in a psalm tells of the joy of having children?
..............................................................................................................
13. What did Peter say about "the end of all things"?.......................
..............................................................................................................
14. To whom did Saul say, "Thou shalt be blind, not seeing the sun for a season"?..............................................................................
15. Who said, "I will give thee the vineyard of Naboth the Jezreel-ite"? ......................................................................................................
16. What Book says, "There is no new thing under the sun"?............
17. What does John say about the love of the world?.......................
..............................................................................................................
18. With what words did Christ set apart the bread of the Lord's supper? .................................................................................................

19. Who said, "The maid is not dead, but sleepeth," and on what occasion? .....................................................................

20. Who said, "When I have a convenient season, I will call for thee"? To whom was he speaking?.................................................

21. What does James say about the belief of devils?..............................
.............................................................................

22. With what words did Christ dedicate the wine of the Lord's supper? .....................................................................

23. What advice does Ecclesiastes give to young people?...................
.............................................................................

24. Who said, "If ye have judged me to be faithful to the Lord, come into my house, and abide there"?...............................................

25. What is Christ's Great Commission?.............................................

## SERIES XXXVI

1. What prophecy did the two angels give of Christ's return?...........
.............................................................................

2. What has Peter to say about holiness?.........................................
.............................................................................

3. What is Christ's requirement of perfection?...................................
.............................................................................

4. In what Book is the sentence, "At evening time it shall be light"?
.............................................................................

5. Who said, "I will not let thee go, except thou bless me"? To whom was he speaking?...............................................

6. Where did the people shout, "The gods are come down to us in the likeness of men"?.............................................

7. In what Book is the expression, "I sleep, but my heart waketh"?
.............................................................................

8. Who asked, "Who hath made man's mouth?" To whom was he speaking?.............................................

9. How is the everlastingness of Christ described in Hebrews?........
.............................................................................

# BIBLE SAYINGS

10. What proverb expresses the reward of liberality?......................

11. How does James contrast doers and hearers?...........................

12. What Psalm verse commends brotherly union?..........................

13. Who said, "Let the dead bury their dead"?................................

14. What verse describes the friendship of David and Jonathan?....

15. Who said, "Hast thou found me, O mine enemy?" To whom was he speaking?...................................................................................

16. What did Peter say about charity?.............................................

17. What, according to Ecclesiastes, is "the conclusion of the whole matter"? ............................................................................................

18. What was Christ's prayer in Gethsemane?.................................

19. What did Christ say about the need of evangelism?...................

20. Who said to Paul, sneeringly, "Almost thou persuadest me to be a Christian"?..........................................................................

21. Who said, "Have thou nothing to do with that just man: for I have suffered many things this day in a dream because of him"? ...................................................................................................

22. What was Peter's boast at the last supper?...............................

23. What did Christ say about confessing him before men?..............

24. What does Ecclesiastes say about the season for things?............

25. What does John say about likeness to God?................................

## SERIES XXXVII

1. In what Book is the prophecy that "HOLINESS TO THE LORD" shall be upon the bells of the horses?................................................

2. Who said, "My son, God will provide himself a lamb for a burnt offering"? To whom did he speak?................................................

3. Who said, "This Jesus hath God raised up, whereof we all are witnesses"? On what occasion?................................................

4. What Psalm verse has to do with the words in our tongues?........
................................................................................................

5. Who said, "God did send me before you to preserve life"? To whom was he speaking?................................................

6. What did Christ command about secret charity?................................
................................................................................................

7. What has Hebrews to say about the temporary nature of this life? ................................................................................................

8. Who said, "As his part is that goeth down to the battle, so shall his part be that tarrieth by the stuff"?................................................

9. Of whom is it said that he "went about doing good"? Who said it? ................................................................................................

10. What did Christ say about peace and a sword?................................
................................................................................................

11. What proverb praises the winning of souls?................................

12. Who said, "Yet now, if thou wilt forgive their sin—; and if not, blot me, I pray thee, out of the book which thou hast written"? To whom was he speaking?................................................

13. Who said that "we must through much tribulation enter into the kingdom of God?................................................

14. What does Job say about his redeemer?................................

15. Who said, "Why are ye fearful, O ye of little faith?" And on what occasion?................................................

16. To whom did Christ say, "O woman, great is thy faith: be it unto thee even as thou wilt"?................................................

# BIBLE SAYINGS

17. What does Peter say, comparing our bodies to grass?..................

............................................................................................

18. Who said at the cross, "Truly this was the Son of God"?...........

19. To whom did Christ say, "Freely ye have received, freely give"?

20. By what test, according to John, may we know that we have passed from death to life?..................

21. When was it said of Jesus, "He could not be hid"?.....................

22. What does James say about every good gift"?...........................

............................................................................................

23. What is the saying in Ecclesiastes about "a living dog?"...........

24. What did the angel say to the women at Christ's tomb?..............

25. What did Peter say about being reproached for Christ?..............

## SERIES XXXVIII

1. What is Peter's addition table?.................................................

............................................................................................

2. What proverb tells what the blessing of the Lord does?.............

............................................................................................

3. What is the greatest verse in the Bible?...................................

............................................................................................

4. Where was Paul when he received the request, "Come over into Macedonia, and help us"?..................

5. What verse of a psalm is a promise of harvest?..........................

............................................................................................

6. What does James say about patience?.......................................

............................................................................................

7. Who said, "The voice is Jacob's voice, but the hands are the hands of Esau"?..................

8. What did Christ command about secret prayer?........................

............................................................................................

9. Who said, "Oh that I were made judge in the land, that every man which hath any suit or cause might come unto me, and I would do him justice!"..................

# BIBLE SAYINGS

10. Who said, "Silver and gold have I none, but such as I have give I thee"? On what occasion?.....................................................................
11. Who said, "My presence shall go with thee, and I will give thee rest"? To whom was he speaking?.......................................................
12. What does James call "the royal law"?.......................................................
13. What picture of heaven begins "They shall hunger no more"?...

...........................................................................................................................

14. Who "exhorted them all, that with purpose of heart they would cleave unto the Lord"?..........................................................................
15. To whom did Christ say, "Son, be of good cheer; thy sins be forgiven thee"?..................................................................................
16. What is said in the Book of Job about acquainting one's self with God?.................................................................................................

...........................................................................................................................

17. What writer advises "the ornament of a meek and quiet spirit"?

...........................................................................................................................

18. Who said of Jesus, "Thou art the Christ, the Son of the living God"? .........................................................................................................
19. What is Christ's saying about sheep, wolves, serpents, and doves? ......................................................................................................

...........................................................................................................................

20. Of whom did Christ say that only one thing was needful, and that she had chosen that good thing?.....................................................
21. What does Ecclesiastes say about vigorous work?.........................

...........................................................................................................................

22. Which of Christ's parables has at the heart of it this sentence, "I will arise and go to my father"?..........................................................
23. What is the cup of cold water verse?.................................................

...........................................................................................................................

24. What great truth did Christ give to the Samaritan woman?......

...........................................................................................................................

25. Who said, "The sceptre shall not depart from Judah, nor a lawgiver from between his feet, until Shiloh come; and unto him shall the gathering of his people be"?.................................................

# BIBLE SAYINGS

## SERIES XXXIX

1. What is James's definition of pure religion?................................
   ..................................................................................................
2. What did Christ say about the revealing of his truth "unto babes"? ...............................................................................
3. Who said, "What profit shall this birthright do to me?"................
   ..................................................................................................
4. What is John's great name for God?........................................
5. What prayer in the Psalms asks God to search the heart?............
   ..................................................................................................
6. Who said of Christ, "There is none other name under heaven given among men whereby we must be saved"? When?............
7. What does Malachi say about God's name being great among the Gentiles?......................................................................
8. Who said, "Unstable as water, thou shalt not excel"? Of whom was he speaking?..........................................................
9. In what Book is the benediction beginning, "Now the God of peace, that brought again from the dead our Lord Jesus"?..........
   ..................................................................................................
10. Repeat the Lord's Prayer.................................................................
    ..................................................................................................
11. What is the saying in Deuteronomy about the nearness of God's word? ...............................................................................
12. What is the proverb about lying lips?...........................................
    ..................................................................................................
13. Who said, "Known unto God are all his works from the beginning of the world"? When did he say it?............................
14. Regarding whom did the people shout, "It is the voice of a god, and not of a man"?....................................................
15. How does Peter state the atonement?........................................
    ..................................................................................................
16. What assurance had Job of the result of his trials?.....................

65

17. What voice came from heaven at Christ's transfiguration?........
18. Complete Christ's saying, "They that be whole need not a physician, but . . ."...............................................................................
19. What threefold name for himself did Christ give to Thomas?....

20. What does Peter advise us to do with our care?............................
21. What definite statement of his diety did Christ give Philip?........

22. What is Christ's command for the troubled?...............................
23. What did Christ say about Christian public speaking?.................
24. How did Christ sum up the teachings of the feeding of the five thousand? ...........................................................................................
25. What does Ecclesiastes say about "the race" and "the battle"?

...........................................................................................................

## SERIES XL

1. What is Peter's prescription for a long and happy life?.............
2. What is Micah's summary of duty?..............................................
3. What is Christ's invitation to the weary?....................................

4. Who said, "This is none other but the house of God, and this is the gate of heaven"? Where was he?......................................
5. What does James say about a double minded man?....................

6. What is the proverb about a false balance?................................

7. What is Christ's saying about his yoke?......................................

8. What verse of a psalm concerns house-building?.......................

9. To whom did God say, "Draw not nigh hither: put off thy shoes from off thy feet, for the place whereon thou standest is holy ground"? What was the place?..............................................

# BIBLE SAYINGS

10. Who said, "Of a truth I perceive that God is no respecter of persons"? .....................................................................................

11. What did God say to Samuel about man's outward appearance"? ..................................................................................

12. Of whom did Christ say, "I have not found so great faith, no, not in Israel"? ....................................................................

13. What prophecy of Zechariah was fulfilled on Palm Sunday? ....
..................................................................................................................

14. To whom did the Lord say, "I have much people in this city"? What was the city? .......................................................................
..................................................................................................................

15. According to John, how may we know that we know God? ........
..................................................................................................................

16. What is Christ's word about eternal bliss and woe? .......................
..................................................................................................................

17. What did Christ say about making ready for us in heaven? ........
..................................................................................................................

18. Who said, "I am not come to call the righteous, but sinners to repentance"? ..........................................................................

19. In what words did Christ announce the coming of the Holy Spirit? .............................................................................................

20. How did Christ define friendship with him? ...............................
..................................................................................................................

21. What has James to say about faith and works? ...........................
..................................................................................................................

22. What is Christ's prayer for Christian union? ...............................
..................................................................................................................

23. What does Ecclesiastes say about casting bread upon the waters? ........................................................................................
..................................................................................................................

24. With what words did Christ restore Peter to full discipleship?
..................................................................................................................

25. What did Christ say that Christians should and should not fear?
..................................................................................................................

## ADDITIONAL STUDIES

### SERIES XLI

### MORE SAYINGS OF CHRIST

1. What saying by Christ is recorded outside the Gospels?............
2. What did Christ say about what goes into the mouth and what comes out of it?......................................................................
3. What is Christ's saying about blind leaders?...............................
4. What did Christ say in pity of the hungry five thousand?..............
5. What did Christ say to his weatherwise critics?............................
6. What did Christ say about losing and saving life?........................
7. What was Christ's saying about the grain of mustard seed?......
.................................................................................................
8. What was Christ's saying about a child's humility?.......................
9. What was Christ's saying about children's angels?.......................
10. What is Christ's word for prayer meetings?................................
11. What did Christ say when Peter asked him whether he should forgive an offence repeated seven times?...............................
12. What did Christ say about the sanctity of the marriage vow?....
.................................................................................................
13. What did Christ say when children were brought to him to bless? ....................................................................................
14. What is Christ's most comprehensive promise regarding prayer? .................................................................................
15. In what words did Christ commend endurance?..........................
16. What is Christ's saying about the carcass and the eagles?............
17. What did the risen Christ say to Thomas?..................................
18. In what words does Christ urge readiness for his coming?..........
.................................................................................................
19. In what words does Christ commend the faithful servant of his parable of the talents?......................................................
20. On the judgment day, how will Christ identify himself with the poor and needy?........................................................................

# BIBLE SAYINGS

21. What did Christ say to the sleepy disciples in Gethsemane?........
...........................................................................................................
22. What did Christ say when Peter used his sword in Gethsemane?
23. What did Christ say about marriage in heaven?.........................
24. Of whom did Christ say that her gifts exceeded all the gifts of the rich men?.........................................................................................
25. What did Christ say about his followers' popularity?..................
26. What did Christ say about false Christs?...................................
27. What did Christ say about the permanence of his words?............
28. What did Christ say about being on guard?................................
29. What did Christ say when Mary anointed him with the precious ointment? ...............................................................................................
30. What did Christ say to Peter when he said he would always be loyal? ...................................................................................................
31. What did Christ say to Peter, after a night of unsuccessful fishing? ..................................................................................................
32. What did Christ say to the fishers after the great haul of fishes?
33. What did Christ say to the palsied man let down through the roof? ....................................................................................................
34. What did Christ say when his critics objected to his associating with publicans and sinners?...............................................................
35. What did Christ say about mingling the new with the old?..........
...........................................................................................................
36. What did Christ say about old wine?..........................................
37. What did Christ say about his authority over the Sabbath?........
38. What woe did Christ pronounce on the rich?.............................
39. What is Christ's woe pronounced on the very popular?................
40. How did Christ describe the reward of generous givers?............
41. What has Christ to say about obedience merely in words?......
...........................................................................................................
42. With what words did Christ raise the son of the widow of Nain?
...........................................................................................................
43. What did Christ say about those who found no fault in him?....
...........................................................................................................

44. What did Christ say about the differing modes of doing God's will? ............................................................................

45. What did Christ say about the sinning woman who anointed his feet? .............................................................................

46. What did Christ say to the healed Gadarene demoniac? ............
................................................................................................

47. What did Christ say about cross-bearing? ................................
................................................................................................

48. What did Christ say to those who were ashamed of him? ............
................................................................................................

49. What did Christ say when some one cast out devils in his name?
................................................................................................

50. What did Christ say when one whom he had called asked first to attend his father's funeral? ..........................................

51. What did Christ say when one whom he had called asked first to say farewell to his home folks? ..........................................

52. What did Christ say when the apostles returned from a successful evangelistic tour? ................................................

53. How did Christ conclude the parable of the good Samaritan? ....
................................................................................................

54. What did Christ say about those who were not with him? ............

55. What did Christ say about forsaking possessions? .......................

56. What did Christ say about heaven's joy over restored sinners?
................................................................................................

57. What did Christ say about the wisdom of worldlings? ...............

58. What did Christ say about the "mammon of unrighteousness"?
................................................................................................

59. What did Christ say about being faithful in little things? ............
................................................................................................

60. In his parable of Dives and Lazarus what did Christ say about the separation between heaven and hell? ................................

61. What did Christ say after the healing of the ten lepers? .............

62. What did Christ say about the secret nature of the kingdom of God? ...........................................................................................

63. What is the conclusion of the parable of the Pharisee and the publican? .............................................................................................

64. What did Christ say to Peter, after telling him that Satan desired to have him?.................................................................................

65. What did Christ say to his disciples as he entered Gethsemane?
.................................................................................................................

66. What were Christ's first words on the cross?................................
.................................................................................................................

67. What did Christ say to the repentant thief on the cross?.............
.................................................................................................................

68. What did Christ say just before dying?............................................
.................................................................................................................

69. What did Christ say to the two from Emmaus?...............................

70. What were Christ's words just before his ascension?.................
.................................................................................................................

71. What was Christ's prophecy of his resurrection?.........................

72. What did Christ tell Nicodemus about regeneration?.................
.................................................................................................................

73. What was Christ's earliest prophecy of his crucifixion? To whom was it made?...........................................................................

74. What did Christ say about the living water?.................................
.................................................................................................................

75. What did Christ say about his joy in his work?............................

76. What did Christ say about the need for evangelism?..................
.................................................................................................................

77. What did Christ say about God's work and his own?.................

78. What did Christ say of the prophecies of himself?.....................

79. What did Christ say to those who sought him after the feeding of the five thousand?.........................................................................

80. What did Christ say was "the work of God"?...............................
.................................................................................................................

81. What did Christ say about eating his flesh and drinking his blood? ...................................................................................................

82. What test of truth did Christ lay down?........................................

83. What did Christ cry on "the great day of the feast"?......................

84. What did Christ say about the woman taken in adultery?............
.........................................................................................................

85. What did Christ say about being the light of the world?............
.........................................................................................................

86. What did Christ say about the drawing power of the cross?........

87. What did Christ say about feet-washing?.......................................
.........................................................................................................

88. What was Christ's new commandment"?.......................................
.........................................................................................................

89. What was Christ's promise of the "greater works"?....................
.........................................................................................................

90. What was Christ's promise of life because of his life?...............

91. What did Christ say the Comforter would do?...............................

92. What did Christ say about his peace?..............................................

93. What is Christ's allegory of the vine and the branches?............
.........................................................................................................

94. What connection did Christ state between prayer and abiding
in him?...........................................................................................

95. What is Christ's saying about "much fruit"?................................
.........................................................................................................

96. What did Christ say about his joy and his disciples'?................
.........................................................................................................

97. What threefold work of the Comforter did Christ name? ........
.........................................................................................................

98. What did Christ say about the Spirit and truth?..........................
.........................................................................................................

99. How does Christ connect prayer and joy?.....................................
.........................................................................................................

100. What saying of Christ's joins tribulation and cheer?...............
.........................................................................................................

101. How does Christ define eternal life?.............................................
.........................................................................................................

# BIBLE SAYINGS

## SERIES XLII

## MORE SAYINGS OF PAUL

1. How did Paul answer the jailer's question, "What must I do to be saved"?......................................................................................

2. What did Paul say about God's use of temples?............................

3. How did Paul contrast the carnal mind and the spiritual mind?
......................................................................................................

4. What did Paul say about "the fashion of this world"?...............

5. What did Paul say about his birthplace?......................................

6. What did Paul say about his conscience?......................................

7. What did Paul say about his obedience to God's call? To whom was he speaking?......................................................................

8. What did Paul say about the publicity of Christ's life? To whom was he speaking?......................................................................

9. Under what circumstances did Paul speak of "God, whose I am, and whom I serve"?......................................................................

10. Who does Paul say are the sons of God?......................................

11. As to their inheritance, what does Paul say that Christians are?
......................................................................................................

12. What does Paul say about the help given us by the Holy Spirit?

13. What is Paul's most helpful verse?................................................

14. What is Paul's predestination verse?............................................

15. What is Paul's conclusion to the faith that God is for us?

16. What does Paul argue as to God's gifts to us?............................

17. What does Paul ask about separation from Christ's love?............

18. How, according to Paul, can we be "more than conquerors"?
......................................................................................................

19. What is Paul persuaded about separation from Christ's love?

20. What does Paul exclaim about the depth of God's riches?........
......................................................................................................

21. What is Paul's saying about the "living sacrifice"?....................

22. What does Paul say about conformity to this world?................

23. In what words does Paul counsel humility?....................................
24. What does Paul say about union in a church?.............................
25. What does Paul say about hating what is evil?............................
26. What does Paul say about putting others before ourselves?........
      ....................................................................................................
27. What is Paul's prescription for industry?..................................
28. What does Paul command regarding sympathy in joy and sorrow? ....................................................................................
29. What does Paul say about paying back injuries?.......................
30. What is Paul's advice about living peaceably?...........................
31. How does Paul say we should treat our enemies?.......................
32. What does Paul say about "the powers that be"?.........................
33. What does Paul say about debts?...............................................
34. What does Paul urge in view of the fact that "the day is at hand"? ....................................................................................
35. What does Paul say about giving account of ourselves?.............
36. How does Paul define the kingdom of God?...............................
37. What does Paul say about bearing others' infirmities?...............
38. What did Paul say about Christ's unselfishness?.........................
39. What does Paul say about the purpose of the Bible?...................
40. What did Paul say about his pioneering enterprise?...................
41. What does Paul say about preaching?.........................................
42. How does Paul distinguish between knowledge and charity?....
      ....................................................................................................
43. What does Paul say about conceit of knowledge?.......................
44. What does Paul say about his own eating of meat consecrated to idols?..................................................................................
45. What does Paul say about his urge to preach?...........................
46. What is Paul's "all things to all men" verse?.............................
47. How does Paul link temperance with mastery?...........................
48. What does Paul say about the mastery of the senses?...............
49. What warning does Paul give to those who think they are all right? ......................................................................................
50. What does Paul say about escape from temptation?...................

74

51. What does Paul say about the communion elements?...................
52. What does Paul say about doing things to God's glory?...............
53. How does Paul summarize the object of the Lord's supper?........
......................................................................................................
54. What did Paul say would be the result if Christ had not risen?
......................................................................................................
55. What did Christ say of a Christian hope confined to this life?
56. How did Paul contrast Adam and Christ?..................................
57. What did Paul say about evil communications?...........................
58. How does Paul contrast our present body with our resurrection body? ................................................................................................
59. With what questions and praise does Paul conclude his resurrection chapter?..........................................................................
60. What is Paul's conclusion of his chapter on immortality?..........
61. What did Paul say about his important work at Ephesus?........
62. What is Paul's saying containing the words, "Quit you like men"? ................................................................................................
63. What is Paul's reconciliation verse?............................................
64. What did Paul say about Christ's being "made sin for us"?........
......................................................................................................
65. What does Paul say about the association of Christians and non-Christians? ..............................................................................
66. What does Paul command Christians who are associated with non-Christians? ..............................................................................
67. How does Paul describe his disturbed state?.............................
68. How does Paul contrast godly sorrow with the sorrow of the world? ........................................................................................
69. What is Paul's account of Christ's riches and poverty?...............
70. How does Paul say that in giving willingness counts more than wealth? ......................................................................................
71. How does Paul say that one should be outwardly honest as well as inwardly?..............................................................................
72. How does Paul contrast the results of liberal and stingy giving?
73. How does Paul urge cheerful giving?............................................

74. How does Paul render thanks for the gift of Christ?.................

75. By what phrase does Paul insist on complete obedience to Christ? .................................................................................

76. How does Paul condemn boastfulness?........................................

77. How did Paul say that God consoled him for his "thorn in the flesh"? .................................................................................

78. With what reflection did Paul "take pleasure in infirmities"?

79. With what words did Paul express his longing to serve the Corinthians? .........................................................................

80. What does Paul say concerning witnesses?...............................

81. What is Paul's benediction that is in most common use in the churches? .............................................................................

82. Finish Paul's saying, "God forbid that I should glory.".............

83. Finish the account of Christ's work begun by Paul with the words, "God, who is rich in mercy—.".......................................

84. What saying of Paul's combines "grace" and "faith"?................

85. What saying of Paul's speaks of Christians as God's workmanship? ....................................................................................

86. How does Paul describe the condition of those who do not know Christ? ...............................................................................

87. How does Paul describe the union of Jew and Gentile in Christ?

88. What was Paul's great prayer for the Ephesians?.......................

89. What is the benediction in Ephesians?........................................

90. How does Paul characterize the "unity of the Spirit"?.................

91. What does Paul say is the sevenfold oneness of Christians?........

    .....................................................................................................

92. What is the goal which Paul sets before the Christian?................

93. What is Paul's characterization of ideal Christian speech?........

94. What is Paul's "new man" verse?................................................

95. Complete Paul's exhortation to truthfulness: "Putting away lying—." .............................................................................

96. What is Paul's prescription for righteous wrath?.......................

97. What is Paul's saying about grieving the Spirit?.........................

98. What reason does Paul give for our being kind to one another?

99. How did Paul express his longing for death?...................................
100. How did Paul urge peace in the church upon the Philippians?

...........................................................................................................
101. How did Paul compare his knowledge of Christ with all things else? .................................................................................................
102. How did Paul express his aim in life?......................................
103. What is Paul's sentence about pressing toward the mark?..........
104. What is Paul's exhortation to rejoice?......................................
105. In what words did Paul forbid anxiety?....................................
106. What is Paul's sentence about the peace that passes understanding? ..................................................................................................
107. What eight things does Paul urge us to think about?...................
108. How does Paul express his contentment?.................................
109. By what means could Paul do all things?...................................
110. What measure of God's supplies does Paul state?.......................
111. Complete this verse: "Strengthened with all might—.".................
112. How does Paul express the immanence of Christ?.....................
113. How did Paul state to the Colossions the deity of Christ?...........
114. Where did Paul bid us fix our affection?....................................
115. What did Paul say about Christians teaching one another?........
116. What did Paul say about using opportunities for evangelism?....
117. What was Paul's prescription for Christian speech?...................
118. What did Paul say about "the spirit of fear"?...............................
119. How did Paul express the confidence of his belief?.......................
120. How did Paul urge Timothy to endure hard things?.....................
121. What advice as to singleness of purpose did Paul give Timothy?

...........................................................................................................
122. What saying of Paul's speaks of "a workman that needeth not to be ashamed"?...............................................................................
123. What did Paul say the scriptures could do for Timothy?..........

...........................................................................................................
124. What does Paul say about the inspiration of the Bible?...............
125. What did Paul say about constant preaching?...................... ....
126. How did Paul sum up his life?............................................................

## SERIES XLIII

### MORE SAYINGS FROM THE PSALMS

1. What is the psalm verse about the city gates?...............................
2. What psalm verse describes the paths of the Lord?...................
3. What verse of the Psalms tells God's secret?..................................
4. What psalm verse is about washing hands?...................................
5. What psalm verse praises "the habitation of thy house"?...........
6. What verse of a psalm describes God as light and salvation?......
7. What, according to a psalm, is the "one desire" of God's children? ................................................................................................
8. What is the psalm verse about hiding in God's pavilion?...........
9. What verse of a psalm is about seeking God's face?.....................
10. What psalm verse tells how God takes the place of a father and mother? .............................................................................................
11. What is the psalm verse about waiting on the Lord?....................
12. What is the psalm verse about "the beauty of holiness"?...........
13. What psalm verse promises strength and peace to God's people? ................................................................................................
14. What psalm verse expresses the brevity of sorrow and of God's anger? ..............................................................................................
15. What verse of a psalm begins, "Be of good courage"?.................
16. What psalm verses speak of the blessedness of God's forgiveness? .............................................................................................
17. What verse of a psalm speaks of confession of sin?.....................
18. What psalm verse describes God as a hiding place?.....................
19. What verse of a psalm tells about God's instruction, teaching, and guidance?.............................................................................
20. Quote the psalm verse which speaks of the sorrows of the wicked. .............................................................................................
21. What psalm verse speaks of the abundance of God's goodness?
22. What verse of a psalm speaks of God as the Lord of the nation?

# BIBLE SAYINGS

23. What psalm verse tells of the eye of the Lord?..............................
24. What verse of a psalm speaks of blessing God at all times?........
..................................................................................................................
25. In what verse does a psalm magnify the Lord?...........................
26. What psalm verse speaks of "this poor man"?...........................
27. What verse of a psalm speaks of an angel camp?.......................
28. What is the psalm verse about tasting God's goodness?...............
29. What psalm verse combines the fear of God with prosperity?..
..................................................................................................................
30. What psalm verse speaks of young lions?...................................
31. What psalm verse urges us to keep our tongues from evil?........
32. Finish the psalm verse which begins "Depart from evil—."........
33. What is the psalm verse for the broken-hearted?.......................
34. What has a psalm to say about the many afflictions of the right-
    eous? ...................................................................................................
35. What psalm verse speaks of God's mercy in the heavens?........
36. What psalm verse speaks of trusting under the shadow of
    God's wings?........................................................................................
37. What verse of a psalm tells of the fountain of life?.......................
38. What is the verse about fretting over wrong?................................
39. What verse speaks of trusting in God and doing good?...............
40. What is the result, according to the psalm, of delighting in
    God? ......................................................................................................
41. What is the verse about committing one's way to God?...............
42. What is the word of the psalm about the meek?...........................
43. What does the psalm say about the little that a righteous man
    has? ......................................................................................................
44. What does the psalm say about "the steps of a good man"?........
45. What had the Psalmist seen in the matter of the beggary of the
    good? ...................................................................................................
46. What in the psalm about the "green bay tree"?...........................
47. What psalm verse begins, "Mark the perfect man"?...................
48. What verse of the psalm prays for a realization of the shortness
    of life? .................................................................................................

49. What is the psalm verse about considering the poor?....................
........................................................................................................

50. What is the water-brooks verse of the Psalms?.........................

51. What is the psalm verse for the disquieted?............................

52. What psalm verse speaks of God's light and truth?...................
........................................................................................................

53. What verse speaks of God's work for our fathers?.......................

54. What psalm verses speak of God as our refuge and strength?....
........................................................................................................

55. What psalm verse speaks of God as making wars to cease?........

56. What psalm verse admonishes us to "be still"?...........................

57. What psalm verses bid us to "walk about Zion"?........................
........................................................................................................

58. What psalm speaks of God as our guide "even unto death"?........
........................................................................................................

59. What is the doorkeeper verse of the Psalms?...............................

60. What is the psalm comparison of God to a sun and shield?........

61. What is the verse about the meeting of mercy and truth?........

62. What verses picture the agelong love of God for his people?...

63. What verse pictures God in relation to time?...............................

64. What verse tells how God knows our sins?..............................

65. What verse states the probable length of our life?....................
........................................................................................................

66. What verse tells us how to number our days?................................

67. What is the Psalmist's prayer for God's beauty and for life results? ...................................................................................................

68. What does the Psalmist say of him "that dwelleth in the secret place of the Most High"?.....................................................................

69. What is the "refuge and fortress" verse of the Psalms?.............

70. Finish the verse: "A thousand shall fall at thy side—.".................

71. What is the verse about the angels' charge?.................................
........................................................................................................

72. Finish the verse, "The Lord reigneth, he is clothed with majesty." ................................................................................................

# BIBLE SAYINGS

73. What are the psalm questions about the ear and the eye?..........
.............................................................................................

74. What is the psalm verse about the "joyful noise"?......................
75. What is the worship invitation of the Psalms?.............................
.............................................................................................

76. What is the "new song" verse of the Psalms?.............................
77. What are the missionary verses of the Psalms?...........................
.............................................................................................

78. What is the psalm verse about "the beauty of holiness"?...........
.............................................................................................

79. What psalm verses speak of a return for all God's benefits?........
.............................................................................................

80. What is the psalm verse that speaks of the death of God's saints?
.............................................................................................

81. Finish the verse, "The Lord is my strength and song—."............
.............................................................................................

82. What does the psalm verse say about "the stone which the build-
ers refused"?................................................................................

83. What is the psalm verse about "the day which the Lord hath
made"? ........................................................................................

84. What does the psalm say about watching one's speech?.............
85. What psalm verse asks why God should consider man?............
.............................................................................................

86. What psalm verses promise ceaseless praise of God?..................
87. What verses speak of God as "full of compassion"?...................
.............................................................................................

88. Finish the verse beginning, "Thou openest thy hand—."............
89. What verse expresses God's perfect righteousness and holiness?
.............................................................................................

90. What verse speaks of God's nearness to all who pray?...............
91. What verse speaks of praise as "comely"?...................................
92. What verse tells about God's healing the brokenhearted?..........
.............................................................................................

93. What psalm verse speaks of "the finest of the wheat"?...............

## SERIES XLIV

## MORE PROVERBS

1. What is the proverb about making one's self rich and poor?........
2. What is the proverb about deferred hope?................................
3. What is the proverb about sparing the rod?................................
4. What proverb speaks of one's own knowledge of one's sorrow?
5. What is the proverb about foolish choices in life?......................
6. What proverb contrasts toil and talk?................................
7. What proverb extols national righteousness?............................
8. What is the proverb about a gentle reply?................................
9. What proverb speaks of a haughty scorner?............................
10. What is the proverb about a good name?................................
11. What proverb associates the rich and poor as God's children?
    ................................................................
12. What proverb urges us to look ahead?................................
13. What proverb urges child-training?................................
14. What proverb expresses the folly of borrowing?......................
15. What silly excuse does a slothful man give?......................
16. What is the proverb about ancient landmarks?............................
17. What proverb praises the man diligent in business?..................
18. What proverb expresses the transitoriness of wealth?............
19. What proverb expresses the power of thought?......................
20. What proverb warns against drunkenness, gluttony, and too much slumber?................................
21. What proverb describes wine "at the last"?......................
22. What is the proverb that praises a right answer?......................
23. What is the proverb about "a little sleep, a little slumber"?........
24. To what does the proverb compare "a word fitly spoken"?......
25. What is the proverb about coals of fire?......................
26. To what does a proverb compare good news from afar?............
27. What are the two proverbs about answering a fool?..................
28. What is the proverb about a man wise in his own conceit?........

# BIBLE SAYINGS

29. What is the proverb about talebearers?.......................................
30. What is the proverb about boasting of what one is going to do?
.........................................................................................................
31. What is the proverb about self-praise?......................................
.........................................................................................................
32. What is the proverb about friendly criticism?...........................
33. What proverb expresses the stimulation of friendship?............
34. What proverb describes the cowardice of evil men?...................
35. What proverb advises against too outspoken speech?................
36. What is the proverb regarding national ideals?...........................
37. What is the proverb about hasty words?.....................................
.........................................................................................................
38. What proverb praises moderate living?.......................................
39. What is the proverb about a virtuous woman?............................
40. What is the proverb about "a woman that feareth the Lord"?
.........................................................................................................

## SERIES XLV

## MORE SAYINGS FROM THE PROPHETS

1. What is Isaiah's saying about the axe and the saw?.....................
2. What is Isaiah's prophecy of the rod and the Branch?...............
3. What is Isaiah's account of the mind of Christ?...........................
4. How does Isaiah portray Christ as a Judge?................................
5. What is Isaiah's picture of the peacefulness of Messiah's reign?
.........................................................................................................
6. What is Isaiah's prophecy of the universality of the knowledge
   of God?..........................................................................................
7. What is Isaiah's song of trust?......................................................
8. What has Isaiah to say about Lucifer?..........................................
9. What has Isaiah to say about "perfect peace"?............................
10. What saying of Isaiah's connects trust and strength?................
11. What woe does Isaiah pronounce on drunkards?.........................

# BIBLE SAYINGS

12. What is Isaiah's saying about erring through **strong drink**?........
13. How does Isaiah describe God's precepts?...................................
14. What is Isaiah's cornerstone verse?...............................................
...............................................................................................................
15. How does Isaiah describe the evil plight of his people?...............
...............................................................................................................
16. What verse of Isaiah urges "returning and rest"?........................
17. What is Isaiah's prophecy of the "hiding place"?........................
18. What does Isaiah say about liberality?......................................
19. What is Isaiah's saying about the work of righteousness?........
...............................................................................................................
20. What is Isaiah's saying about sowing widely?............................
21. What has Isaiah to say about the prosperity of the righteous?
...............................................................................................................
22. What is Isaiah's prophecy of seeing God and heaven?...........
23. What is Isaiah's picture of the blossoming desert?...................
24. What is Isaiah's message to strengthen the weak?...................
...............................................................................................................
25. What is Isaiah's prophecy of bodily restorations?...................
26. What is Isaiah's highway prophecy?...........................................
27. What is Isaiah's prophecy of the return from exile?.................
28. What is Isaiah's prophecy of the remnant?...............................
29. What are Isaiah's comfort verses?...............................................
...............................................................................................................
30. What is Isaiah's valley prophecy?...............................................
31. What prophecy of Isaiah's brings in the grass?.......................
32. What is Isaiah's shepherd prophecy?.........................................
...............................................................................................................
33. What is Isaiah's measurement verse?.........................................
34. What verse of Isaiah begins, "Hast thou not known?".................
...............................................................................................................
35. What verse of Isaiah tells how God strengthens the weak?........
36. What is Isaiah's eagle verse?.........................................................
37. What is Isaiah's verse of neighborly helpfulness?.......................

# BIBLE SAYINGS

38. What verse in Isaiah begins with "Fear thou not; for I am with thee"? ..................................................................................

39. What verse of Isaiah tells of God holding our right hand?........

40. What is Isaiah's prophecy of the Messiah's marred visage?........
......................................................................................................

41. What is Isaiah's prophecy of the Messiah's lack of beauty?........
......................................................................................................

42. What is Isaiah's prophecy of the rejection of Christ?.................

43. What are Isaiah's three great verses describing the atonement?
......................................................................................................

44. What is Isaiah's prophecy of Christ's silence at his trial?............

45. What is Isaiah's prophecy of Christ's crucifixion with robbers and burial in a rich man's tomb?..................................................

46. What is Isaiah's exhortation to enlargement and enterprise?
......................................................................................................

47. What does Isaiah say about the permanence of God's kindness as compared with the mountains?..............................................

48. What does Isaiah say about the education of children?..............
......................................................................................................

49. What is Isaiah's invitation to the thirsty?..................................
......................................................................................................

50. What is Isaiah's warning against unsatisfying toil?...................
......................................................................................................

51. What is the verse about the everlasting covenant?......................

52. What is Isaiah's intimation that it may some day be too late to seek the Lord?.................................................................................

53. What is Isaiah's promise of pardon to repentant sinners?........
......................................................................................................

54. What does Isaiah say about God's thoughts being higher than man's? ..................................................................................................

55. How does Isaiah compare the fruitfulness of God's word to the fruitfulness of nature?......................................................................

56. What does Isaiah say about the humble dwelling with God?
......................................................................................................

57. What does Isaiah say about the wicked and peace?....................
.........................................................................................................
58. What kind of fast does Isaiah recommend?................................
.........................................................................................................
59. How does Isaiah say we should spend the Sabbath?..................
.........................................................................................................
60. What reason does Isaiah give why God will not hear sinners?
.........................................................................................................
61. How does Isaiah picture the glory of God's children?.............
.........................................................................................................
62. How does Isaiah speak of the coming ingathering into God's kingdom? ....................................................................................
63. What does Isaiah say is the fate of the nation that will not serve God? ..............................................................................................
64. What new names does Isaiah give to the walls and gates of Jerusalem? ...............................................................................................
65. What does Isaiah prophesy shall be the light of God's people?
.........................................................................................................
66. What does Isaiah foretell concerning the mourning of God's people? ...........................................................................................
67. What does Isaiah prophesy concerning the growth of God's people? ...........................................................................................
68. What beautiful verses of Isaiah did Christ use for the text of his sermon at Nazareth?..............................................................
69. What is the rest of the first three verses of that chapter?...........
.........................................................................................................
70. What is Isaiah's watchmen verse?..................................................
71. What verse pictures Messiah's loneliness?..................................
72. What saying pictures the Messiah's sympathy with his people's affliction? .............................................................................................
73. What verse of Isaiah portrays the Lord as our Maker?...............
.........................................................................................................
74. What verse of Jeremiah describes the time when all shall know the Lord?..............................................................................................

# BIBLE SAYINGS

75. What was Jeremiah bidden to say to Baruch?...........................
76. What verse in Lamentations is applied to the crowd that mocked Christ's crucifixion?................................................
77. What is said, in the Lamentations, of God's compassions?........

...............................................................................................
78. What is said in the Lamentations about the young bearing yokes? ...................................................................................
79. What does Amos say about the necessity for prophesying?........

...............................................................................................
80. With what solemn words does Amos announce immediate judgment? ..............................................................................
81. How does Amos characterize the oppressors of his day?............

...............................................................................................
82. In urging men to seek God, what noble account of him does Amos give?...................................................................................
83. How does Amos describe the unpopularity of reformers?..........

...............................................................................................
84. What fate of the oppressors of the poor does Amos foretell?

...............................................................................................
85. On what terms did Amos say that the people might find God gracious again? ..............................................................................
86. How did Amos describe the new righteousness he longed to see?

...............................................................................................
87. What is Amos's woe on the self-satisfied?.................................
88. How did Amos describe his occupation and his call to be a prophet? ...............................................................................
89. What prophet said, "It is better for me to die than to live"?

...............................................................................................
90. What famous prophecy of Isaiah does Micah repeat?...............

...............................................................................................
91. What is Micah's verse about the vine and fig tree?......................
92. What is Micah's prophecy of Bethlehem?..................................
93. What is Malachi's command to return to God?...........................

...............................................................................................

94. What does Malachi say about robbing God?...............................
.................................................................................................

95. What promise does Malachi extend to the tithe-payer?.............
.................................................................................................

96. What is Malachi's prophecy of God's book of remembrance?
.................................................................................................

97. What is Malachi's prophecy of the day when God will make
up his jewels?.........................................................................

98. What is Malachi's prophecy of the rising of the Sun of righteousness? ..............................................................................

99. What is Malachi's prophecy of John the Baptist?......................
.................................................................................................

100. What is the last verse of the Old Testament?.............................
.................................................................................................

## SERIES I

1. Nebuchadnezzar. Dan. 4:30.
2. "To leave the other undone." Luke 11:42.
3. Elihu. Job 32:7.
4. Moses. Ex. 14:14.
5. Ps. 100:1. "Make a joyful noise unto the Lord, all ye lands."
6. Said by the angel to Zacharias, of John the Baptist.
7. Rev. 13:8.
8. Gamaliel. Acts 5:38, 39.
9. Adam. Gen. 2:24.
10. "Ye shall be free indeed." John 8:36.
11. Moses. Lev. 24:20.
12. The tongue. Jas. 3:8.
13. "Thee to repentance." Rom. 2:4.
14. "By prayer and fasting." Mark 9:29.
15. Paul. Titus 2:13.
16. David. Ps. 15:4.
17. Nehemiah. Neh. 4:14.
18. Solomon's Song 8:7.
19. God, at Christ's baptism. Matt. 3:17.
20. Paul. Eph. 5:16.
21. Isaiah. Isa. 42:4.
22. "A word spoken in due season." Prov. 15:23.
23. "The things which God hath prepared for them that love him." 1 Cor. 2:9.
24. Christ. Matt. 12:36.
25. "Your sanctification." 1 Thess. 4:3.

## SERIES II

1. "Consent thou not," Prov. 1:10.
2. John the Baptist's. Matt. 3:10.
3. Jeremiah. Jer. 6:14.
4. "Honor thy father and mother," Eph. 6:2.
5. David. Ps. 56:8.
6. Adam. Gen. 3:12.
7. Habakkuk. Hab. 1:13.
8. The Pharisees. Luke 11:43.
9. "Surely in vain the net is spread in the sight of any bird." Prov. 1:17.
10. Solomon. 1 Chron. 28:9.
11. The Virgin Mary. Luke 1:38.
12. "The things of the Spirit of God." 1 Cor. 2:14.
13. "Enter into his gates with thanksgiving." Ps. 100:4.
14. Saul. 1 Sam. 10:11, 12.
15. Job. Job 38:2.
16. "Bring my sons from far, and my daughters from the ends of the earth." Isa. 43:6.
17. "If the salt have lost his saltness, wherewith will ye season it?" Mark 9:50.
18. "He is able to succor them that are tempted." Heb. 2:18.
19. "Thou shalt find him, if thou seek him with all thy heart and with all thy soul." Deut. 4:29.
20. "Before Abraham was, I am." John 8:58.
21. "There is no respect of persons with God." Rom. 2:11.
22. "Pride goeth before destruction, and an haughty spirit before a fall." Prov. 16:18.
23. "And none shall make you afraid." Lev. 26:6.
24. Ps. 61:2.
25. Daniel to Belshazzar. Dan. 5:17.

## SERIES III

1. Moses. Ex. 14:15.
2. Mary's. Luke 1:52.
3. "The letter killeth, but the spirit giveth life." 2 Cor. 3:6.
4. "And a thousand years as one day." 2 Pet. 3:8.
5. "Than that thou shouldest vow and not pay." Eccl. 5:5.
6. Deut. 6:4.
7. Job. Job 2:10.
8. "The fathers have eaten sour grapes, and the children's teeth are set on edge." Ezek. 18:2.
9. "Whosoever shall do the will of my father which is in heaven." Matt. 12:50.
10. By faith in Christ Jesus." Gal. 3:26.
11. "Blessed are the dead which die in the Lord from henceforth: Yea, saith the Spirit, that they may rest from their labors; and their works do follow them." Rev. 14:13.

12. "Pleasant words are as an honey-comb, sweet to the soul, and health to the bones." Prov. 16:24.
13. "My expectation is from him." Ps. 62:5.
14. To Adam, by God. Gen. 3:19.
15. "And of Gideon." Judg. 7:18.
16. The apostles. Acts 6:4.
17. Christ. Mark 10:9.
18. "Unto thee shall all flesh come." Ps. 65:2.
19. Nehemiah. Neh. 6:3.
20. "Lean not unto thine own under-standing." Prov. 3:5.
21. "As a thief in the night." 1 Thess. 5:2.
22. The Old Testament men and women of faith. Heb. 11:38.
23. "Ephraim is joined to idols: let him alone." Hos. 4:17.
24. "Learn to do well." Isa. 1:16, 17.
25. "The night cometh, when no man can work." John 9:4.

SERIES IV

1. "Teachest thou not thyself?" Rom. 2:21.
2. Esther. Esth. 4:16.
3. "And he will direct thy paths." Prov. 3:6.
4. David, of Abner. 2 Sam. 3:38.
5. "Whosoever shall confess me be-fore men, him shall the Son of man also confess before the angels of God." Luke 12:8.
6. "And thy paths drop fatness." Ps. 65:11.
7. Moses, after the passage of the Red Sea. Ex. 15:11.
8. "And stablisheth a city by in-iquity!" Hab. 2:12.
9. "I am the light of the world." John 9:5.
10. "While it is called To-day." Heb. 3:13.
11. James. Jas. 3:18.
12. Isaiah. Isa. 44:22.
13. "Slow to anger, and plenteous in mercy." Ps. 103:8.
14. The Shunammite. 2 Kings 4:13.
15. Paul. 1 Cor. 3:6.
16. Job. Job 3:17.

17. God, of Christ, at his baptism. Matt. 3:17.
18. "Always in a good thing." Gal. 4:18.
19. Stephen, before the Sanhedrin. Acts 7:22.
20. "If it be found in the way of right-eousness." Prov. 16:31.
21. Jeremiah. Jer. 8:20.
22. "Ye cannot serve God and mam-mon." Matt. 6:24.
23. The Revelation. Rev. 1:11.
24. Daniel's, to Belshazzar. Dan. 5:27.
25. "So far hath he removed our trans-gressions from us." Ps. 103:12.

SERIES V

1. "Striving against sin." Heb. 12:4.
2. Stephen. Acts 7:48.
3. Cain. Gen. 4:9.
4. Moses. Deut. 34:7.
5. "And renew a right spirit within me." Ps. 51:10.
6. "To come unto me, and forbid them not: for of such is the king-dom of God." Mark 10:14.
7. Christ. Rev. 1:18.
8. "He correcteth." Prov. 3:12.
9. The Queen of Sheba, concerning Solomon's wisdom and splendor. 1 Kings 10:7.
10. "In thy presence is fulness of joy; at the right hand there are pleas-ures for evermore." Ps. 16:11.
11. "And the body than raiment?" Matt. 6:25.
12. Paul. Rom. 3:4.
13. Jeremiah. Jer. 8:22.
14. The Lord, to Job. Job 38:7.
15. Nehemiah. Neh. 6:11.
16. The man born blind whom Christ healed. John 9:25.
17. "Blessed be the Lord, who daily loadeth us with benefits." Ps. 68:19.
18. Cain. Gen. 4:13.
19. Paul. 1 Tim. 2:5.
20. Christ, to Peter and Andrew. Matt. 4:19.
21. Hosea. Hos. 6:3.
22. "In the abundance of the things which he possesseth." Luke 12:15.
23. Ezekiel. Ezek. 18:20.

24. Joshua. Josh. 1:7.
25. "As the waters cover the sea." Hab. 2:14.

## SERIES VI

1. "The zeal of thine house hath eaten me up." Ps. 69:9; John 2:17.
2. "I desired mercy, and not sacrifice; and the knowledge of God more than burnt offerings." Hos. 6:6.
3. "Whom the Lord loveth he chasteneth, and scourgeth every son whom he receiveth." Heb. 12:6.
4. "Enoch walked with God: and he was not; for God took him." Gen. 5:24.
5. Isaiah. Isa. 45:9.
6. "And in her left hand riches and honor." Prov. 3:16.
7. The rich young ruler. Mark 10:17.
8. "There is liberty." 2 Cor. 3:17.
9. Rev. 15:3.
10. "And my mouth shall show forth thy praise." Ps. 51:15.
11. Miriam's, after the crossing of the Red Sea. Ex. 15:21.
12. Joshua. Josh. 1:8.
13. Jeremiah, "the weeping prophet." Jer. 9:1.
14. Habakkuk. Hab. 2:15.
15. "For theirs is the kingdom of heaven." Matt. 5:3.
16. "Stand fast therefore in the liberty wherewith Christ hath made us free, and be not entangled again with the yoke of bondage." Gal. 5:1.
17. The public Bible reading of Ezra and Nehemiah. Neh. 8:8.
18. Gideon's. Judg. 8:4.
19. "Like as a father pitieth his children, so the Lord pitieth them that fear him." Ps. 103:13.
20. In the parable of the foolish rich man. Luke 12:19.
21. "Faith which worketh by love." Gal. 5:6.
22. "Reap the same." Job 4:8.
23. Ezekiel. Ezek. 18:31.
24. "He that entereth not by the door into the sheepfold, but climbeth up some other way, the same is a thief and a robber." John 10:1.

25. Wisdom is the principal thing; therefore get wisdom: and with all thy getting get understanding." Prov. 4:7.

## SERIES VII

1. "Consider the lilies of the field, how they grow; they toil not, neither do they spin: and yet I say unto you, That even Solomon in all his glory was not arrayed like one of these." Matt. 6:29.
2. "But is longsuffering to usward, not willing that any should perish, but that all should come to repentance." 2 Pet. 3:9.
3. Esther. Esth. 5:6.
4. "All thine heart, and with all thy soul, and with all thy might." Deut. 6:5.
5. "A friend loveth at all times." Prov. 17:17.
6. "And they shall reap the whirlwind." Hos. 8:7.
7. "Putting on the breastplate of faith and love; and for an helmet, the hope of salvation." Hos. 5:8.
8. "Though your sins be as scarlet, they shall be as white as snow; though they be red like crimson, they shall be as wool." Isa. 1:18.
9. The Virgin Mary. Luke 1:53.
10. Paul. Rom. 3:10, 12.
11. "Be filled with the Spirit." Eph. 5:18.
12. "Keep me as the apple of the eye, hide me under the shadow of thy wings." Ps. 17:8.
13. David. 2 Sam. 5:24.
14. God. Job 38:11.
15. King Darius's. Dan. 6:8.
16. "Ye are God's husbandry, ye are God's building." 1 Cor. 3:9.
17. "For they shall be comforted." Matt. 5:4.
18. Of King Saul. 1 Sam. 10:27.
19. God, before the flood. Gen. 6:3.
20. Elisha, of the Shunammite. 2 Kings 4:26.
21. Eccl. 5:9.
22. Christ. Matt. 13:9.
23. "The church of the living God, the

pillar and ground of the truth."
1 Tim. 3:15.

24. David. 1 Chron. 29:14.

25. "We hold the beginning of our confidence stedfast unto the end." Heb. 3:14.

### SERIES VIII

1. "Nevertheless afterward it yieldeth the peaceable fruit of righteousness." Heb. 12:11.

2. Rehoboam, son of Solomon. 1 Kings 12:10.

3. James. Jas. 4:3.

4. Moses. Num. 10:35.

5. That of Ephesus. Rev. 2:4.

6. The Israelites. Lev. 26·8.

7. "The path of the just is as the shining light, that shineth more and more unto the perfect day." Prov. 4:18.

8. "All ye ends of the earth." Isa. 45:14.

9. "Blessed are the meek: for they shall inherit the earth." Matt. 5:5.

10. "And come short of the glory of God." Rom. 3:23.

11. "A merry heart doeth good like a medicine." Prov. 17:22.

12. Ezekiel. Ezek. 21:27.

13. King Ahasuerus. Esth. 6:6.

14. "To give the light of the knowledge of the glory of God in the face of Jesus Christ." 2 Cor. 4:6.

15. Of John the Baptist. Luke 1:66.

16. Isaiah. Isa. 2:4.

17. Nehemiah and Ezra. Neh. 8:10.

18. Moses. Num. 12:3.

19. Job. Job 38:31.

20. "And all these things shall be added unto you." Matt. 6:33.

21. Rev. 16:16.

22. Paul. 1 Thess. 5:10.

23. "A broken spirit: a broken and a contrite heart, O God, thou wilt not despise." Ps. 51:17.

24. The manna. Ex. 16:15.

25. Zacharias. Luke 1:78.

### SERIES IX

1. "Whosoever hath not, from him shall be taken away even that he hath." Matt. 13:12.

2. "He shall be saved, and shall go in and out, and find pasture." John 10:9.

3. "And the little hills, by righteousness." Ps. 72:3.

4. Of the days before the flood. Gen. 6:4.

5. Heb. 3:15.

6. Stephen. Acts 7:56.

7. The rich young ruler. Mark 10:21.

8. Hosea. Hos. 10:13.

9. That he "shall not be satisfied with silver." Eccl. 5:10.

10. "The Lord is my rock, and my fortress, and my deliverer; my God, my strength, in whom I will trust; my buckler, and the horn of my salvation, and my high tower." Ps. 18:2.

11. Solomon. 2 Chron. 1:10.

12. "They shall be filled." Matt. 5:6.

13. "Other foundation can no man lay than that is laid, which is Jesus Christ." 1 Cor. 3:11.

14. "Keep thy heart with all diligence; for out of it are the issues of life." Prov. 4:23.

15. David. 2 Sam. 6:9.

16. "Thou shalt bind them for a sign upon thine hand, and they shall be as frontlets between thine eyes." Deut. 6:8.

17. Jeremiah. Jer. 10:23.

18. "Ye fathers, provoke not your children to wrath, but bring them up in the nurture and admonition of the Lord." Eph. 6:4.

19. The church in Smyrna. Rev. 2:10.

20. "Be strong and of good courage; be not afraid, neither be thou dismayed: for the Lord thy God is with thee whithersoever thou goest." Josh. 1:9.

21. Daniel. Dan. 6:22.

22. Christ. Luke 12:30.

23. Paul. 1 Tim. 3:16.

24. "We, according to his promise, look for new heavens and a new earth, wherein dwelleth righteousness." 2 Pet. 3:13.

25. "As for man, his days are as grass: as a flower of the field, so he flourisheth." Ps. 103:15.

## SERIES X

1. To Elisha. 2 Kings 4:40.
2. "Shall a man be more pure than his maker?" Job 4:17.
3. "Let all the earth keep silence before him." Hab. 2:20.
4. "Blessed are the merciful: for they shall obtain mercy." Matt. 5:7.
5. "A little leaven leaveneth the whole lump." Gal. 5:9.
6. "God resisteth the proud, but giveth grace unto the humble." Jas. 4:6.
7. "Drink waters out of thine own cistern, and running waters out of thine own well." Prov. 5:15.
8. "He sent from above, he took me." Ps. 18:16.
9. Rehoboam, son of Solomon. 1 Kings 12:11.
10. Christ. Matt. 13:16.
11. Paul. 1 Thess. 5:15.
12. Saul. 1 Sam. 11:13.
13. "And the feeble knees; and make straight paths for your feet." Heb. 12:12.
14. Jephthah. Judg. 11:31.
15. "Even to your old age I am he; and even to hoar hairs will I carry you." Isa. 46:4.
16. Stephen. Acts 7:59.
17. The parable of the sower. Matt. 13:21.
18. "Is counted wise." Prov. 17:28.
19. God, after the flood. Gen. 8:22.
20. Samuel. 1 Sam. 12:3.
21. Rev. 19:6.
22. Paul. Rom. 4:25.
23. "Upon them that fear him, and his righteousness unto children's children." Ps. 103:17.
24. The manna. Ex. 16:18.
25. "The inspiration of the Almighty giveth them understanding." Job 32:8.

## SERIES XI

1. "With bands of love." Hos. 11:4.
2. "The good shepherd giveth his life for the sheep." John 10:11.
3. Rev. 2:17.
4. Joshua. Josh. 3:8.

5. "And his kingdom ruleth over all." Ps. 103:19.
6. "Take therefore no thought for the morrow: for the morrow shall take thought for the things of itself. Sufficient unto the day is the evil thereof." Matt. 8:34.
7. "Every creature of God is good, and nothing to be refused, if it be received with thanksgiving." 1 Tim. 4:4.
8. The ten cowardly spies. Num. 13:28.
9. The prayer of the Levites. Neh. 9:17.
10. "Blessed are the pure in heart, for they shall see God." Matt. 5:8.
11. "The fire shall try every man's work of what sort it is." 1 Cor. 3:13.
12. The heroes of faith of the Old Testament. Heb. 11:34.
13. Deut. 6:9.
14. "The fool hath said in his heart, There is no God." Ps. 53:1.
15. "Yet I will rejoice in the Lord, I will joy in the God of my salvation." Hab. 3:17, 18.
16. "So is he that layeth up treasure for himself, and is not rich toward God." Luke 12:21.
17. "He will flee from you." Jas. 4:7.
18. An Ephraimite. Judg. 12:6.
19. Isaiah's. Isa. 2:5.
20. "How hard is it for them that trust in riches to enter into the kingdom of God!" Mark 10:24.
21. Paul. 1 Thess. 5:16.
22. Jeremiah. Jer. 13:23.
23. "And envy slayeth the silly one." Job. 5:2.
24. "They are increased that eat them." Eccl. 5:11.
25. Stephen. Acts 7:60.

## SERIES XII

1. Of Mary and Joseph. Luke 2:7.
2. Solomon in dedicating the temple. 2 Chron. 6:18.
3. Noah and his sons. Gen. 9:6.
4. "He shall judge the poor of the people, he shall save the children

of the needy, and shall break in pieces the oppressor." Ps. 72:4.

5. "Go to the ant, thou sluggard; consider her ways, and be wise." Prov. 6:6.

6. "Yet the inward man is renewed day by day." 2 Cor. 4:16.

7. John. 1 John 1:5.

8. The king of Israel, when Naaman came to be cured of leprosy. 2 Kings 5:7

9. Ezekiel, on the death of his wife. Ezek. 24:16.

10. "Judge not, that ye be not judged." Matt. 7:1.

11. "Thou shalt love thy neighbor as thyself." Gal. 5:14.

12. Job. Job 42:5.

13. Obed-edom. 2 Sam. 6:12.

14. "Not with eyeservice, as men-pleasers; but as servants of Christ, doing the will of God from the heart." Eph. 6:6.

15. "Blessed are the peacemakers: for they shall be called the children of God." Matt. 5:9.

16. "For thou wilt light my candle: the Lord my God will enlighten my darkness." Ps. 18:28.

17. Jeroboam and his followers. 1 Kings 12:16.

18. Paul. 1 Thess. 5:17.

19. Dan. 7:22, and elsewhere in Daniel.

20. "Because of unbelief." Heb. 3:19.

21. Caleb. Num. 13:30.

22. "And who is a rock save our God?" Ps. 18:31.

23. "Even so know I the Father." John 10:15.

24. "Therefore being justified by faith, we have peace with God through our Lord Jesus Christ." Rom. 5:1.

25. Zephaniah. 3:17.

## SERIES XIII

1. David. 2 Sam. 6:14.

2. "Blessed are they which are persecuted for righteousness' sake: for theirs is the kingdom of heaven." Matt. 5:10.

3. "Know ye not that ye are the temple of God, and that the Spirit of God dwelleth in you?" 1 Cor. 3:16.

4. Dan. 12:2.

5. "For it is your Father's good pleasure to give you the kingdom." Luke 12:32.

6. Rev. 19:9.

7. "And the Lord alone shall be exalted in that day." Isa. 2:11.

8. Nehemiah. Neh. 13:11.

9. "It is easier for a camel to go through the eye of a needle, than for a rich man to enter into the kingdom of God." Mark 10:25.

10. Simon the sorcerer. Acts 8:10.

11. "Yet a little sleep, a little slumber, a little folding of the hands to sleep: so shall thy poverty come as one that travelleth, and thy want as an armed man." Prov. 6:10, 11.

12. Jethro, Moses' father-in-law, after the exodus. Ex. 18:11.

13. "The sparks fly upward." Job 5:7.

14. "As to the Lord, and not to men." Eph. 6:7.

15. "Other sheep I have, which are not of this fold: them also I must bring." John 10:16.

16. "And whose heart departeth from the Lord." Jer. 17:5.

17. "I do set my bow in the cloud, and it shall be for a token of a covenant between me and the earth." Gen. 9:13.

18. "Walk in the Spirit, and ye shall not fulfil the lust of the flesh." Gal. 5:16.

19. "If we walk in the light, as he is in the light, we have fellowship one with another, and the blood of Jesus Christ his son cleanseth us from all sin." 1 John 1:7.

20. "We have this treasure in earthen vessels, that the excellency of the power may be of God, and not of us." 2 Cor. 4:7.

21. "And the firmament showeth his handywork." Ps. 19:1.

22. "The righteous runneth into it, and is safe." Prov. 18:10.

23. King Asa. 2 Chron. 14:11.

24. Isa. 48:22.

25. To the shepherds at Bethlehem. Luke 2:10.

## SERIES XIV

1. "The care of this world, and the deceitfulness of riches, choke the word, and he becometh unfruitful." Matt. 13:22.
2. Paul. 1 Thess. 5:18.
3. Ezekiel. Ezek. 33:9.
4. "He shall come down like rain upon the mown grass: as showers that water the earth." Ps. 72:6.
5. Deut. 6:16.
6. "Why beholdest thou the mote that is in thy brother's eye, but considerest not the beam that is in thy own eye?" Matt. 7:3.
7. "Bodily exercise profiteth little: but godliness is profitable unto all things, having promise of the life that now is, and of that which is to come." 1 Tim. 4:8.
8. Naaman's servants. 2 Kings 5:13.
9. "The sleep of a laboring man is sweet, whether he eat little or much: but the abundance of the rich will not suffer him to sleep." Eccl. 5:12.
10. Moses. Ex. 19:4.
11. Joshua's cairn commemorating the passage of the Jordan. Josh. 4:21.
12. That of Sardis. Rev. 3:1.
13. Ps. 104:16.
14. Samson. Judg. 14:14.
15. "And from the river unto the ends of the earth." Ps. 72:8.
16. Christ. Matt. 5:13.
17. "To the people of God." Heb. 4:9.
18. Elijah. 1 Kings 17:4.
19. Heb. 12:14.
20. "In wisdom hast thou made them all." Ps. 104:24.
21. "Where your treasure is, there will your heart be also." Luke 12:34.
22. "And he will draw nigh to you." Jas. 4:8.
23. Haggai. Hag. 1:4.
24. "I will sing praise to my God while I have my being." Ps. 104:33.
25. Jeremiah. Jer. 17:7.

## SERIES XV

1. "Our light affliction, which is but for a moment, worketh for us a far more exceeding and eternal weight of glory." 2 Cor. 4:17.
2. "Be ye therefore ready also: for the Son of man cometh in an hour when ye think not." Luke 12:40.
3. Isaiah. Isa. 2:22.
4. Nehemiah. Neh. 13:17.
5. Paul. Eph. 6:10.
6. Christ. Mark 10:27.
7. Nimrod. Gen. 10:9.
8. "The testimony of the Lord is sure, making wise the simple." Ps. 19:7.
9. Ezekiel. Ezek. 33:11.
10. Paul's. 1 Thess. 5:19.
11. "That they may see your good works, and glorify your Father which is in heaven." Matt. 5:16.
12. Azariah. 2 Chron. 15:2.
13. To the Israelites, through Moses. Ex. 19:6.
14. Heb. 12:23.
15. Simon the scorcerer. Acts 8:20.
16. Christ. John 10:16.
17. "And forsake not the law of thy mother." Prov. 6:20.
18. "Despise not thou the chastening of the Almighty." Job 5:17.
19. "He shall lift you up." Jas. 4:10.
20. An angel, speaking to the shepherds. Luke 2:11.
21. Isaiah. Isa. 49:6.
22. Hosea. Hos. 13:14.
23. Paul. Rom. 5:3, 4.
24. Christ. Matt. 13:29.
25. Eccl. 6:7.

## SERIES XVI

1. "I have the power to lay it down, and I have the power to take it again." John 10:18.
2. To Moses at Sinai. Ex. 19:8.
3. "The poor also, and him that hath no helper." Ps. 72:12.
4. That it is "foolishness with God." 1 Cor. 3:19.
5. "We deceive ourselves, and the truth is not in us." 1 John 1:8.
6. "Humility." Prov. 18:12.
7. At the building of the Tower of Babel. Gen. 11:4.
8. Isaiah. Isa. 3:24.
9. "Give not that which is holy unto

the dogs, neither cast ye your pearls before swine." Matt. 7:6.

10. Timothy. 1 Tim. 4:12.
11. Philadelphia. Rev. 3:8.
12. "All nations shall call him blessed." Ps. 72:17.
13. At the beginning of the Ten Commandments. Ex. 20:2.
14. "They that be wise shall shine as the brightness of the firmament; and they that turn many to righteousness as the stars for ever and ever." Dan. 12:3.
15. Christ. Mark. 10:31.
16. "In due time Christ died for the ungodly." Rom. 5:6.
17. "The word of God is quick, and powerful, and sharper than any twoedged sword, piercing even to the dividing asunder of soul and spirit, and of the joints and marrow, and is a discerner of the thoughts and intents of the heart." Heb. 4:12.
18. "Who walk in the law of the Lord." Ps. 119:1.
19. Naaman. 2 Kings 5:18.
20. "He that earneth wages earneth wages to put it into a bag with holes." Hag. 1:6.
21. Christ. Luke 12:48.
22. "The flesh lusteth against the Spirit, and the Spirit against the flesh: and these are contrary the one to the other: so that ye cannot do the things that ye would." Gal. 5:17.
23. The widow of Zarephath. 1 Kings 17:14.
24. Joshua and Caleb. Num. 14:9.
25. John, in the Revelation. Rev. 19:16.

## SERIES XVII

1. Moses. Deut. 8:2.
2. The angels, at Bethlehem. Luke 2:14.
3. Paul. Rom. 5:8.
4. His wife Michal. 2 Sam. 6:20.
5. "Life and death are in the power of the tongue." Prov. 18:21.
6. "Ask, and it shall be given you; seek, and ye shall find; knock, and

it shall be opened unto you." Matt. 7:7.

7. Samson. Judg. 14:18.
8. "By taking heed thereto according to thy word." Ps. 119:9.
9. "For what is your life? It is even a vapor, that appeareth for a little time, and then vanisheth away." Jas. 4:14.
10. The man with a drawn sword, to Joshua. Josh. 5:14.
11. Isaiah. Isa. 49:10.
12. Christ. John 12:50.
13. "Hold fast that which is good." 1 Thess. 5:21.
14. "Thou shalt have no other gods before me." Ex. 20:3.
15. "My days are swifter than a weaver's shuttle, and are spent without hope." Job 7:6.
16. "More to be desired are they than gold, yea, than much fine gold: sweeter also than honey and the honeycomb." Ps. 19:10.
17. James and John. Mark 10:38.
18. "We look not at the things which are seen, but at the things which are not seen: for the things which are seen are temporal; but the things which are not seen are eternal." 2 Cor. 4:18.
19. "I saw a new heaven and a new earth; for the first heaven and the first earth were passed away; and there was no more sea." Rev. 21:1.
20. "Say unto him, Take away all iniquity, and receive us graciously: so will we render the calves of our lips." Hos. 14:2.
21. "And afterward receive me to glory." Ps. 73:24.
22. "For righteousness, but behold a cry." Isa. 5:7.
23. "How much more shall your Father which is in heaven give good things to them that ask him?" Matt. 7:11.
24. "All are yours; and ye are Christ's; and Christ's is God's. 1 Cor. 3:22, 23.
25. Peter, to Simon the scorcerer. Acts 8:23.

## SERIES XVIII

1. "It is better to go to the house of mourning, than to the house of feasting: for that is the end of all men; and the living will lay it to his heart." Eccl. 7:2.
2. Abraham. Gen. 12:2.
3. "My sheep hear my voice, and I know them, and they follow me." John 10:27.
4. Timothy. 1 Tim. 4:14.
5. "That I might not sin against thee." Ps. 119:11.
6. "Thou shalt not make unto thee any graven image," etc. Ex. 20:4-6.
7. Deut. 8:18.
8. "And his clothes not be burned?" Prov. 6:27.
9. The parable of the tares. Matt. 13:43.
10. "So by the obedience of one shall many be made righteous." Rom. 5:19.
11. "To him it is sin." Jas. 4:17.
12. Simeon, when he was presented in the temple. Luke 2:29.
13. "The heart is deceitful above all things, and desperately wicked: who can know it?" Jer. 17:9.
14. Moses, at Meribah. Num. 20:10.
15. "A man that hath friends must show himself friendly: and there is a friend that sticketh closer than a brother." Prov. 18:24.
16. "Till heaven and earth pass, one jot or one tittle shall in no wise pass from the law, till all be fulfilled." Matt. 5:18.
17. "Love, joy, peace, longsuffering, gentleness, goodness, faith, meekness, temperance." Gal. 5:22, 23.
18. "I will shake all nations, and the desire of all nations shall come: and I will fill this house with glory." Hag. 2:7.
19. The girdle of truth, the breastplate of righteousness, the sandals of peace, the shield of faith, the helmet of salvation, and "the sword of the Spirit, which is the word of God." Eph. 6:13-17.
20. "I will take away the stony heart out of your flesh, and I will give you an heart of flesh." Ezek. 36:26.
21. Job. Job 7:16.
22. "And filleth the hungry soul with goodness." Ps. 107:9.
23. Samson. Judg. 15:16.
24. Heb. 4:15.
25. Laodicea. Rev. 3:16.

## SERIES XIX

1. "In the beginning was the Word, and the Word was with God, and the Word was God." John 1:1.
2. Amos. Amos 8:5.
3. King Ahab to Elijah. 1 Kings 18:17.
4. "He is faithful and just to forgive us our sins, and to cleanse us from all unrighteousness." 1 John 1:9.
5. Hanani. 2 Chron. 16:9.
6. Joshua, referring to Jericho. Josh. 6:16.
7. Heb. 12:29.
8. Christ. John 18:36.
9. Elisha, speaking to Gehazi. 2 Kings 5:27.
10. Joseph's brothers, referring to Joseph. Gen. 37:19.
11. "Let the words of my mouth, and the meditation of my heart, be acceptable in thy sight, O Lord, my strength, and my redeemer." Ps. 19:14.
12. Christ. Luke 13:3.
13. Paul. Phil. 1:21.
14. Rev. 21:4.
15. Job. Job 9:2.
16. "Thou shalt not take the name of the Lord thy God in vain." Ex.20:7.
17. Moses. Deut. 11:26.
18. Isaiah. Isa. 5:21.
19. "If thy right eye offend thee, pluck it out, and cast it from thee." Matt. 5:29.
20. "Reckon ye also yourselves to be dead indeed unto sin, but alive unto God through Jesus Christ our Lord." Rom. 6:11.
21. "Bind them upon thy fingers, write them upon the table of thine heart." Prov. 7:3.

22. "God is the strength of my heart, and my portion forever." Ps. 73:26.
23. "But to minister, and to give his life a ransom for many." Mark 10:45.
24. Hosea. Hos. 14:4.
25. "That I may behold wondrous things out of thy law." Ps. 119:18.

## SERIES XX

1. Christ. Matt. 5:34.
2. Paul. 1 Tim. 5:8.
3. Simeon, of the Virgin Mary. Luke 2:35.
4. David. Ps. 20:5.
5. Abraham, to Lot. Gen. 13:9.
6. Micaiah. 2 Chron. 18:7.
7. Jeremiah. Jer. 17:4.
8. "To this end was I born, and for this cause came I into the world, that I should bear witness unto the truth." John 18:37.
9. "We have a building of God, an house not made with hands, eternal in the heavens." 2 Cor. 5:1.
10. Ezekiel's vision of the river from the sanctuary. Ezek. 47:9.
11. "Remember the sabbath day, to keep it holy," etc. Ex. 20:8-11.
12. "Lendeth unto the Lord." Prov. 19:17.
13. Christ. Matt. 13:46.
14. "It is required in stewards, that a man be found faithful." 1 Cor. 4.2.
15. "Strive to enter in at the strait gate: for many, I say unto you, will seek to enter in, and shall not be able." Luke 13:24.
16. To the crackling of thorns under a pot. Eccl. 7:6.
17. Amos. Amos 8:11.
18. Ps. 107:23.
19. The men of Gibeon, because of their deceit. Josh. 9:21.
20. Isaiah. Isa. 30:4.
21. "I and the Father are one." John 10:30.
22. "He that overcometh shall inherit all things; and I will be his God, and he shall be my son." Rev. 21:7.

23. "O how love I thy law! it is my meditation all the day." Ps. 119:97.
24. Judg. 16:30.
25. Philip, to the Ethiopian treasurer. Acts 8:30.

## SERIES XXI

1. Elisha, surrounded by the Syrian army. 2 Kings 6:16.
2. Haggai. Hag. 2:8.
3. Christ. Luke 13:32.
4. "Bear ye one another's burdens, and so fulfil the law of Christ." "For every man shall bear his own burden." Gal. 6:2, 5.
5. "All things whatsoever ye would that men should do to you, do ye even so to them." Matt. 7:12.
6. Job 11:7.
7. Elijah. 1 Kings 18:21.
8. The Israelites, just before the plague of fiery serpents. Num. 21:5.
9. Paul. 1 Thess. 5:22.
10. Ps. 20:1-4.
11. "That we may receive mercy, and find grace to help in time of need." Heb. 4:16.
12. Joseph, to Potiphar's wife. Gen. 39:9.
13. "Honor thy father and thy mother," etc. Ex. 20:12.
14. James. Jas. 5:11.
15. At Nazareth. Matt. 13:57.
16. Obadiah 4.
17. "Thy word is a lamp unto my feet, and a light unto my path." Ps. 119:105.
18. "They shall obtain gladness and joy; and sorrow and mourning shall flee away." Isa. 51:11.
19. Deut. 18:15.
20. Jehoshaphat. 2 Chron. 19:11.
21. "Wisdom is better than rubies; and all the things that may be desired are not to be compared to it." Prov. 8:11.
22. Pilate, of Christ. John 19:5.
23. Christ, to Saul. Acts 9:5.
24. "Who is so great a God as our God?" Ps. 77:13.
25. Jeremiah. Jer. 20:14.

## SERIES XXII

1. Hosea. Hos. 14:8.
2. Christ. John 10:37.
3. "But in lowliness of mind let each esteem other better than themselves." Phil. 2:3.
4. Abraham. Gen. 13:15.
5. "The fear of the Lord." Ps. 111:10.
6. Ezekiel. Ezek. 47:12.
7. "Whatsoever is more than these cometh of evil." Matt. 5:37.
8. Saul. Acts 9:6.
9. "Yet learned he obedience by the things which he suffered." Heb. 5:8.
10. "Woe unto them that join house to house, that lay field to field, till there be no place, that they may be placed alone in the midst of the earth!" Isa. 5:8.
11. Joshua. Josh. 10:12.
12. "Thou shalt not kill." Ex. 20:13.
13. "It giveth understanding unto the simple." Ps. 119:130.
14. Blind Bartimæus. Mark 10:47.
15. "Let him that is taught in the word communicate unto him that teacheth in all good things." Gal. 6:6.
16. "Say not thou, What is the cause that the former days were better than these?" Eccl. 7:10.
17. Naomi, to Ruth and Orpah. Ruth 1:8.
18. "All things were made by him, and without him was not anything made that was made." John 1:3.
19. The king of Sodom. Gen. 14:23.
20. Balaam. Num. 23:8.
21. Joel 2:13.
22. "And shalt believe in thine heart that God hath raised him from the dead, thou shalt be saved." Rom. 10:9.
23. "For the Lord God Almighty and the Lamb are the temple of it." Rev. 21:22.
24. Joseph. Gen. 40:8.
25. John the Baptist, to Herod Antipas, concerning Herodias. Matt. 14:4.

## SERIES XXIII

1. Christ. Luke 11:41.
2. Paul. 1 Thess. 2:12.
3. Isa. 65:24.
4. Samuel. 1 Sam. 7:12.
5. David. Ps. 14:1.
6. Nebuchadnezzar. Dan. 4:3.
7. Peter and John. Acts 4:20.
8. John. Rev. 11:15.
9. Christ, to the father of the demoniac son. Mark 9:23.
10. The Creator. Gen. 1:3.
11. Num. 6:24-26.
12. Christ. Matt. 12:30.
13. Paul. Eph. 5:2.
14. James. Jas. 3:5.
15. Hos. 2:15.
16. Solomon. 1 Kings 3:7.
17. Joshua. Josh. 24:15.
18. The wise-men. Matt. 2:2.
19. Paul. Rom. 1:16.
20. Heb. 2:3.
21. Isa. 42:3.
22. Ps. 50:10.
23. Elisha, of Elijah. 2 Kings 2:12.
24. Job. Job 1:21.
25. To Ezekiel. Ezek. 3:17.

## SERIES XXIV

1. Christ. John 8:32.
2. Paul. 1 Cor. 1:27.
3. The Lord through Moses concerning the passover. Ex. 12:14.
4. Job. Job 28:28.
5. Christ. Mark 16:15.
6. Song of Solomon 6:10.
7. Paul. Gal. 2:20.
8. David. Ps. 55:6.
9. Micah. Mic. 7:19.
10. Paul. 1 Tim. 1:15.
11. David, on the death of Saul and Jonathan. 2 Sam. 1:19.
12. Ps. 97:10.
13. Eccl. 3:14.
14. Paul. 2 Cor. 1:20.
15. Prov. 15:3.
16. John the Baptist. Matt. 3:2.
17. Paul. Titus 1:15.
18. Moses to Joshua. Deut. 3:22.
19. Ps. 150:6.
20. Moses. Heb. 11:27.
21. Lev. 10:10.

22. David, when his three warriors brought him water from the well of Bethlehem. 1 Chron. 11:19.
23. Peter. 2 Pet. 1:20.
24. Ezra. Ezra 7:10.
25. Jude 24, 25.

## SERIES XXV

1. King Ahasuerus. Esth. 1:22.
2. Moses, of Asher. Deut. 34:25.
3. Solomon. Prov. 1:7.
4. Christ. Matt. 12:34.
5. Paul, to the Thessalonians. 1 Thess. 4:11.
6. Satan, of Job. Job 2:4.
7. The Creator. Gen. 1:26.
8. David. Ps. 98:4.
9. Jeremiah, when called to be a prophet. Jer. 1:6.
10. The father of the demoniac child, to Christ. Mark 9:24.
11. Rev. 12:11.
12. Hosea. Hos. 4:6.
13. Habakkuk. Hab. 2:4. Quoted several times by Paul.
14. Peter, to Ananias. Acts 5:4.
15. Prov. 15:20.
16. Moses, to the Israelites, just before crossing the Red Sea. Ex. 14:13.
17. Moses. Deut. 4:24.
18. The angel Gabriel, to the Virgin Mary. Luke 1:28.
19. Paul. 2 Cor. 3:5.
20. Nehemiah. Neh. 4:6.
21. David. Ps. 55:22.
22. Christ. Luke 12:7.
23. Lev. 19:30.
24. Solomon. 1 Kings 8:30.
25. John the Baptist. Matt. 3:8.

## SERIES XXVI

1. John. Rev. 1:5, 6.
2. Ezekiel. Ezek. 8:12.
3. Christ. John 8:44.
4. David. Ps. 51:7.
5. David, of Jonathan. 2 Sam. 1:26.
6. Eccl. 4:12.
7. Paul, to the Corinthians. 1 Cor. 2:2.
8. David. Ps. 16:6.
9. God. Gen. 2:18.

10. Deborah and Barak. Judg. 5:20.
11. Paul. Rom. 2:1.
12. The children of Bethel, to Elisha. 2 Kings 2:23.
13. Isa. 43:2.
14. Nahum 1:7.
15. Paul. Eph. 5:14.
16. Samuel, to Saul. 1 Sam. 10:6.
17. Job. Job 31:17.
18. Song of Solomon 8:6.
19. Christ. John 8:51.
20. 1 Tim. 1.17.
21. I ter. 2 Pet. 2:9.
22. Heb. 12:1, 2.
23. Moses. Deut. 33:27.
24. Mordecai to Esther. Esth. 4:14.
25. Peter and the other apostles. Acts 5:29.

## SERIES XXVII

1. Christ, when left behind in the temple at the age of twelve. Luke 3:49.
2. Paul. 1 Cor. 4:20.
3. John. Rev. 21:23.
4. "Wine is a mocker, strong drink is raging: and whosoever is deceived thereby is not wise." Prov. 20:1.
5. The four lepers who discovered the departure of the Syrians. 2 Kings 7:9.
6. Christ, concerning the ass's colt. Mark 11:3.
7. "The wages of sin is death; but the gift of God is eternal life through Jesus Christ our Lord." Rom. 6:23.
8. James. Jas. 5:15.
9. "Some trust in chariots, and some in horses: but we will remember the name of the Lord our God." Ps. 20:7.
10. Samuel. 1 Sam. 12:17.
11. Job. Job 12:2.
12. Paul. 2 Cor. 5:6.
13. Pilate. John 18:38.
14. Zech. 3:8.
15. Paul. 2 Thess. 3:1.
16. After Elijah's sacrifice on Mt. Carmel. 1 Kings 18:39.
17. "My God, my God, why hast thou forsaken me?" Ps. 22:1.
18. "O Jerusalem, Jerusalem, . . . how

often would I have gathered thy children together, as a hen doth gather her brood under her wings, and ye would not!" Luke 13:34.

19. "Godliness with contentment is great gain." 1 Tim. 6:6.

20. "Ye shall know them ¹ their fruits. Do men gather grapes of thorns or figs of thistles?" Matt. 7:16.

21. "Whosoever shall call upon the name of the Lord shall be saved." Rom. 10:13.

22. Christ. John 10:38.
23. 1 Cor. 13.
24. Joab. 2 Sam. 10:12.
25. Rev. 21:27.

## SERIES XXVIII

1. "In the day of prosperity be joyful, but in the day of adversity consider: God also hath set the one over against the other, to the end that man should find nothing after him." Eccl. 7:14.
2. Balaam. Num. 24:17.
3. Job. Job 13:15.
4. "And the life was the light of men." John 1:4.
5. Paul. 1 Cor. 14:40.
6. Ananias, concerning Saul. Acts 9:15.
7. Joel. Joel 2:28.
8. Ps. 79:13.
9. "Thou shalt not commit adultery." Ex. 20:14.
10. The seraphim in Isaiah's vision. Isa. 6:3.
11. The multitude, in Christ's triumphal entry. Mark 11:9.
12. "Leaveneth the whole lump." 1 Cor. 5:6.
13. Pilate, refusing to change the title on Christ's cross. John 19:22.
14. Isaiah, when called to be a prophet. Isa. 6:8.
15. To Abraham, in promising that Sarah should have a child in her old age. Gen. 18:14.
16. "Intreat me not to leave thee," etc. Ruth 1:16, 17.
17. "Whosoever shall smite thee on

thy right cheek, turn to him the other also." Matt. 5:39.

18. "Be not forgetful to entertain strangers: for thereby some have entertained angels unawares." Heb. 13:2.

19. "That which I do I allow not: for what I would, that do I not; but what I hate, that do I." Rom. 7:15.

20. "Whosoever exalteth himself shall be abased; and he that humbleth himself shall be exalted." Luke 14:11.

21. To Jonah, during the great storm. Jonah 1:6.

22. "The Lord's name is to be praised." Ps. 113:3.

23. "And into the patient waiting for Christ." 2 Thess. 3:5.

24. Of Lazarus. John 11:4.

25. "Divers weights, and divers measures, both of them are alike an abomination to the Lord." Prov. 20:10.

## SERIES XXIX

1. "Even a child is known by his doings, whether his work be pure, and whether it be right." Prov. 20:11.
2. Christ. Matt. 7:20.
3. Peter. Acts 9:40.
4. Pharaoh's chief butler, remembering his promise to Joseph of two years before. Gen. 41:9.
5. Deut. 19:21.
6. Elisha's servant, after the sacrifice on Carmel. 1 Kings 18:44.
7. Christ. Matt. 14:16.
8. Christ. Rev. 3:19.
9. "This we commanded you, that if any would not work, neither should he eat." 2 Thess. 3:10.
10. Ps. 119:165.
11. "Thou shalt not steal." Ex. 20:15.
12. Hazael. 2 Kings 8:13.
13. "The Lord is my shepherd," etc.
14. Solomon's Song 2:1.
15. Christ, in the parable of the marriage feast. Matt. 22:8.
16. Paul. Rom. 10:14.
17. Rev. 22:11.
18. Isaiah. Isa. 52:7.

19. Joshua. Josh. 23:10.
20. "And those that seek me early shall find me." Prov. 8:17.
21. Paul. 2 Cor. 5:7.
22. Christ. Luke 3:7.
23. "For whatsoever a man soweth, that shall he also reap." Gal. 6:7.
24. Nathan. 2 Sam. 12:3, 4.
25. Christ, to his mother, with reference to John. John 19:26.

SERIES XXX

1. In Zechariah. Zech. 3:10.
2. Jonathan. 1 Sam. 14:6.
3. Jeremiah. Jer. 29:13.
4. "But every man also on the things of others." Phil. 2:4.
5. Christ. Mark 11:17.
6. Isa. 7:14.
7. King Jotham of Judah. 2 Chron. 27:6.
8. Paul. 1 Tim. 6:10.
9. "Thou shalt not bear false witness against thy neighbor." Ex. 20:16.
10. Job. Job 14:1.
11. "Leaving the principles of the doctrine of Christ." Heb. 6:1.
12. "The effectual fervent prayer of a righteous man availeth much." Jas. 5:16.
13. "Go out into the highways and hedges, and compel them to come in, that my house may be filled." Luke 14:23.
14. Nathan to David. 2 Sam. 12:7.
15. "And the fulness thereof; the world, and they that dwell therein." Ps. 24:1.
16. Jonah. Jonah 2:3.
17. Paul. 1 Cor. 5:7.
18. "Grace and truth came by Jesus Christ." John 1:17.
19. Moses. Deut. 2:3.
20. The king in Christ's parable of the marriage feast. Matt. 22:12.
21. Peter. Acts 10:15.
22. Joel 3:14.
23. Joseph. Gen. 41:16.
24. Samuel, to Saul. 1 Sam. 15:22.
25. Peter. Luke 5:5.

SERIES XXXI

1. Joshua. Josh. 23:14.

2. "It is naught, it is naught, saith the buyer: but when he is gone his way, then he boasteth." Prov. 20:14.
3. Zechariah. Zech. 4:6.
4. "Whosoever shall compel thee to go a mile, go with him twain." Matt. 5:41.
5. Of Paul and Silas at Thessalonica. Acts 17:6.
6. Paul. Phil. 2:5.
7. Job. "All the days of my appointed time will I wait, till my change come." Job 14:14.
8. "Thou shalt not covet," etc. Ex. 20:17.
9. Jehu the son of Nimshi. 2 Kings 9:20.
10. "I will lift up mine eyes unto the hills." Ps. 121:1.
11. "Have seen a great light." Isa. 9:2.
12. The risen Lord, to Mary Magdalene. John 20:17.
13. Timothy. 1 Tim. 6:12.
14. "If any man hear my voice, and open the door, I will come in to him, and will sup with him, and he with me." Rev. 3:20.
15. Jeremiah. Jer. 31:3.
16. "But he that doeth the will of my Father which is in heaven." Matt. 7:21.
17. "He which converteth the sinner from the error of his way shall save a soul from death, and shall hide a multitude of sins." Jas. 5:20.
18. "They sold the righteous for silver, and the poor for a pair of shoes." Amos 2:6.
19. Abraham, when God proposed to destroy Sodom. Gen. 18:25.
20. Eccl. 7:29.
21. Christ, walking to the disciples on the sea. Matt. 14:27.
22. Paul. Rom. 7:24.
23. Peter. 1 Pet. 1:8.
24. "He hath heard my voice and my supplications." Ps. 116:1.
25. Solomon's Song 2:4.

SERIES XXXII

1. "Believe that ye receive them, and ye shall have them." Mark 11:24.
2. "Faith cometh by hearing, and

hearing by the word of God." Rom. 10:17.

3. "The Spirit and the Bride say, Come. And let him that heareth say, Come. And let him that is athirst come. And whosoever will, let him take of the water of life freely." Rev. 22:17.

4. King Hezekiah, of Sennacherib. 2 Chron. 32:8.

5. "He that sinneth against me wrongeth his own soul: all they that hate me love death." Prov. 8:36.

6. Christ. Matt. 22:14.

7. Paul. 1 Cor. 15:3.

8. "After the power of an endless life." Heb. 7:16.

9. "He should have fed them also with the finest of the wheat: and with honey out of the rock should I have satisfied thee." Ps. 81:16.

10. John the Baptist. John 1:29.

11. Paul. 2 Cor. 5:14.

12. "The grace of our Lord Jesus Christ be with you all. Amen." Rev. 22:21.

13. "When thou shalt vow a vow unto the Lord thy God, thou shalt not slack to pay it." Deut. 23:21.

14. "Mercy and truth shall go before thy face." Ps. 89:14.

15. "Let us not be weary in well doing: for in due season we shall reap, if we faint not." Gal. 6:9.

16. To Martha, just before raising Lazarus. John 11:25.

17. "Buried with him in baptism." Col. 2:12.

18. "My soul longeth, yea, even fainteth for the courts of the Lord: my heart and my flesh crieth out for the living God." Ps. 84:1.

19. Paul. 2 Thess. 3:13.

20. Amos. Amos 3:3.

21. Heb. 13:4.

22. Lot. Gen. 19:20.

23. "If any man come to me, and hate not his father, and mother, and wife, and children, and brethren, and sisters, yea, and his own life also, he cannot be my disciple." Luke 14:26.

24. "There is therefore now no condemnation to them which are in Christ Jesus, who walk not after the flesh, but after the Spirit." Rom. 8:1.

25. "Give to him that asketh thee, and from him that would borrow of thee turn not thou away." Matt. 5:42.

## SERIES XXXIII

1. Pharaoh. Gen. 41:38.

2. Samuel, speaking to Saul. 1 Sam. 15:26.

3. "I will; be thou clean." Matt. 8:3.

4. Col. 2:21.

5. Paul. Rom. 11:29.

6. On meeting his disciples in the upper room after the resurrection. John 20:19.

7. "When the Lord shall bring again Zion." Isa. 52:8.

8. Moses, after the giving of the Ten Commandments. Ex. 20:20.

9. "They shall walk, O Lord, in the light of thy countenance." Ps. 89:15.

10. Jonah. Jonah 3:4.

11. Peter, after the great haul of fishes. Luke 5:8.

12. "Let us do good unto all men, especially unto them who are of the household of faith." Gal. 6:10.

13. Job, to his three friends. Job 16:2.

14. Deut. 25:4.

15. "Unto us a child is born, unto us a son is given: and the government shall be upon his shoulder: and his name shall be called Wonderful, Counsellor, The Mighty God, The Everlasting Father, The Prince of Peace." Isa. 9:6.

16. "Render to Cæsar the things that are Cæsar's, and to God the things that are God's." Mark 12:17.

17. Peter, when worshipped in the house of Cornelius. Acts 10:26.

18. "That they be not high-minded, nor trust in uncertain riches," etc. 1 Tim. 6:17-19.

19. Christ to Peter, as he was sinking in the waves. Matt. 14:31.

20. Zechariah. Zech. 4:10.

21. After his exile and repentance. 2 Chron. 33:13.
22. "The Lord is thy shade upon thy right hand." Ps. 121:5.
23. Sarah, when Isaac was born. Gen. 21:6.
24. Jeremiah. Jer. 31:33.
25. "In the resurrection they neither marry, nor are given in marriage, but are as the angels of God in heaven." Matt. 22:30.

## SERIES XXXIV

1. Andrew. John 1:41.
2. "To receive power, and riches, and wisdom, and strength, and honor, and glory, and blessing." Rev. 5:12.
3. "He that hath clean hands, and a pure heart; who hath not lifted up his soul unto vanity, nor sworn deceitfully." Ps. 24:4.
4. David, on the death of his child by Bath-sheba. 2 Sam. 12:23.
5. "Lo, the winter is past, the rain is over and gone; the flowers appear on the earth; the time of the singing of birds is come, and the voice of the turtle is heard in our land; the fig tree putteth forth her green figs, and the vines with the tender grape give a good smell." Solomon's Song 2:11-13.
6. Paul. 1 Cor. 15:10.
7. Christ, at the raising of Lazarus. John 11:43.
8. John. 1 John 2:2.
9. Jehu to Jonadab. 2 Kings 10:16.
10. "Love your enemies, bless them that curse you, do good to them that hate you, and pray for them which despitefully use you, and persecute you." Matt. 5:44.
11. Peter. 1 Pet. 2:13.
12. The Bereans. Acts 17:11.
13. Eccl. 8:8.
14. "All men are liars." Ps. 116:11.
15. "Know ye not that your body is the temple of the Holy Ghost which is in you, which ye have of God, and ye are not your own? For ye are bought with a price: therefore glorify God in your body, and in your spirit, which are God's. 1 Cor. 6:19, 20.
16. "Lest thou come to poverty." Prov. 20:13.
17. "Be not ye called Rabbi: for one is your Master, even Christ; and all ye are brethren." Matt. 23:8.
18. "If any man be in Christ, he is a new creature: old things are passed away; behold, all things are become new." 2 Cor. 5:17.
19. "They that trust in the Lord shall be as Mt. Zion, which cannot be removed, but abideth forever." Ps. 125:1.
20. "Be content with such things as ye have: for he hath said, I will never leave thee, nor forsake thee." Heb. 13:5.
21. "The fear of the Lord." Prov. 9:10.
22. "Work out your own salvation with fear and trembling, for it is God which worketh in you both to will and to do of his good pleasure." Phil. 2: 12, 13.
23. "The streets of the city shall be full of boys and girls playing in the streets thereof." Zech. 8:5.
24. Aaron. Ex. 32:24.
25. Samuel. 1 Sam. 15:29.

## SERIES XXXV

1. "He maketh his sun to rise on the evil and on the good, and sendeth rain on the just and on the unjust." Matt. 5:45.
2. "It is not for you to know the times or the seasons, which the Father hath put in his own power." Acts 1:7.
3. "In that day there shall be a fountain opened, to the house of David and to the inhabitants of Jerusalem for sin and for uncleanness." Zech. 13:1.
4. Song of Solomon 2:15.
5. Laban to Jacob. Gen. 31:49.
6. Christ. Matt. 8:20.
7. God, to Moses. Ex. 3:14.
8. "Blessed is the man that endureth temptation: for when he is tried,

he shall receive the crown of life, which the Lord hath promised to them that love him." Jas. 1:12.

9. "Where no counsel is, the people fall: but in the multitude of counsellors there is safety." Prov. 11:14.

10. David, to Goliath. 1 Sam. 17:47.

11. "The very hairs of your head are all numbered." Matt. 10:30.

12. "Happy is the man that hath his quiver full of them." Ps. 127:5.

13. "The end of all things is at hand: be ye therefore sober, and watch unto prayer." 1 Pet. 4:7.

14. Elymas the sorcerer. Acts 13:11.

15. Jezebel. 1 Kings 21:7.

16. Ecclesiastes (1:9).

17. "If any man love the world, the love of the Father is not in him." 1 John 2:15.

18. "Take, eat; this is my body." Matt. 26:26.

19. Christ, when he raised the daughter of Jairus. Matt. 9:24.

20. Felix, to Paul. Acts 24:25.

21. "The devils also believe, and tremble." Jas. 2:19.

22. "Drink ye all of it; for this is my blood of the new testament, which is shed for many for the remission of sins." Matt. 26:28.

23. "Remember now thy Creator in the days of thy youth." Eccl. 12:1.

24. Lydia. Acts 16:15.

25. "All power is given unto me in heaven and in earth. Go ye therefore, and teach all nations, baptizing them in the name of the Father, and of the Son, and of the Holy Ghost: teaching them to observe all things whatsoever I have commanded you: and, lo, I am with you alway, even unto the end of the world. Amen." Matt. 28:18-20.

## SERIES XXXVI

1. "This same Jesus, which is taken up from you into heaven, shall so come in like manner as ye have seen him go into heaven." Acts 1:11.

2. "As he which hath called you is holy, so be ye holy in all manner of conversation." 1 Pet. 1:15.

3. "Be ye therefore perfect, even as your Father which is in heaven is perfect." Matt. 5:48.

4. Zech. 14:7.

5. Jacob, to the angel by the Jabbok. Gen. 32:26.

6. At Lystra. Acts 14:11.

7. Song of Solomon 5:2.

8. God, to Moses. Ex. 4:11.

9. "Jesus Christ, the same yesterday, and to-day, and forever." Heb. 13:8.

10. "The liberal soul shall be made fat: and he that watereth shall be watered also himself." Prov. 11:25.

11. "Be ye doers of the word, and not hearers only, deceiving your own selves." Jas. 1:22.

12. "Behold, how good and how pleasant it is for brethren to dwell together in unity!" Ps. 133:1.

13. Christ. Matt. 8:22.

14. "The soul of Jonathan was knit with the soul of David, and Jonathan loved him as his own soul." 1 Sam. 18:1.

15. King Ahab, to Elijah. 1 Kings 21:20.

16. "Charity shall cover the multitude of sins." 1 Pet. 4:8.

17. "Fear God, and keep his commandments: for this is the whole duty of man." Eccl. 12:13.

18. "O my Father, if it be possible, let this cup pass from me: nevertheless not as I will, but as thou wilt." Matt. 26:39.

19. "The harvest truly is plenteous, but the laborers are few." Matt. 9:37.

20. King Agrippa II. Acts 26:28.

21. Pilate's wife. Matt. 27:19.

22. "Though I should die with thee, yet will I not deny thee." Matt. 26:35.

23. "Whosoever therefore shall confess me before men, him will I confess also before my Father which is in heaven." Matt. 10:32.

24. "To everything there is a season,

and a time to every purpose under the heaven." Eccl. 3:1.

25. "Beloved, now are we the sons of God, and it doth not yet appear what we shall be: but we know that, when he shall appear, we shall be like him; for we shall see him as he is." 1 John 3:2.

## SERIES XXXVII

1. Zech. 14:20.
2. Abraham, speaking to Isaac. Gen. 22:8.
3. From Peter's sermon at Pentecost. Acts 2:32.
4. "There is not a word in my tongue, but lo, O Lord, thou knowest it altogether." Ps. 139:4.
5. Joseph, to his brothers. Gen. 45:5.
6. "When thou doest alms, let not thy left hand know what thy right hand doeth." Matt. 6:3.
7. "Here have we no continuing city, but we seek one to come." Heb. 13:14.
8. David. 1 Sam. 30:24.
9. Of Christ; said by Peter. Acts 10:38.
10. "Think not that I am come to send peace on earth: I came not to send peace, but a sword." Matt. 10:34.
11. "The fruit of the righteous is a tree of life; and he that winneth souls is wise." Prov. 11:30.
12. Moses, to God. Ex. 32:32.
13. Paul. Acts 14:22.
14. "I know that my redeemer liveth, and that he shall stand at the latter day upon the earth." Job. 19:25.
15. Christ, in the great storm on the sea. Matt. 8:26.
16. To the Syro-phœnician woman. Matt. 15:28.
17. "All flesh is as grass, and all the glory of man as the flower of grass. The grass withereth, and the flower thereof falleth away: but the word of the Lord endureth forever." 1 Pet. 1:24, 25.
18. The Roman centurion and soldiers. Matt. 27:54.

19. To the twelve apostles. Matt. 10:8.
20. "We know that we have passed from death unto life, because we love the brethren." 1 John 3: 14.
21. When he sought retirement near Tyre and Sidon. Mark 7:24.
22. "Every good gift and every perfect gift is from above, and cometh down from the Father of lights, with whom is no variableness, neither shadow of turning." Jas. 1:17.
23. "A living dog is better than a dead lion." Eccl. 9:4.
24. "Fear not ye: for I know that ye seek Jesus, which was crucified. He is not here: for he is risen, as he said. Come, see the place where the Lord lay." Matt. 28: 5, 6.
25. "If ye be reproached for the name of Christ, happy are ye." 1 Pet. 4:14.

## SERIES XXXVIII

1. "And beside this, giving all diligence, add to your faith virtue," etc. 2 Pet. 1: 5-7.
2. "The blessing of the Lord, it maketh rich, and he addeth no sorrow with it." Prov. 10:22.
3. "God so loved the world, that he gave his only begotten Son, that whosoever believeth in him should not perish, but have everlasting life." John 3:16.
4. At Troas. Acts 16:9.
5. "He that goeth forth and weepeth, bearing precious seed, shall doubtless come again with rejoicing, bringing his sheaves with him." Ps. 126:6.
6. "Let patience have her perfect work, that ye may be perfect and entire, wanting nothing." Jas. 1:4.
7. Isaac. Gen. 27:22.
8. "But thou, when thou prayest, enter into thy closet, and when thou hast shut thy door, pray to thy Father which is in secret; and thy Father which seeth in secret shall reward thee openly." Matt. 6:6.
9. Absalom. 2 Sam. 15:4.

10. Peter, in healing the cripple. Acts 3:6.
11. God, to Moses. Ex. 33:14.
12. "Thou shalt love thy neighbor as thyself." Jas. 2:8.
13. "They shall hunger no more, neither thirst any more; neither shall the sun light on them, nor any heat. For the Lamb which is in the midst of the throne shall feed them, and shall lead them unto living fountains of waters: and God shall wipe away all tears from their eyes." Rev. 7:16, 17.
14. Barnabas. Acts 11:23.
15. To the Capernaum paralytic. Matt. 9:2.
16. "Acquaint now thyself with him, and be at peace; thereby good shall come unto thee." Job 22:21.
17. Peter. 1 Pet. 3:4.
18. Peter. Matt. 16:16.
19. "Behold, I send you forth as sheep in the midst of wolves; be ye therefore wise as serpents, and harmless as doves." Matt. 10:16.
20. Of Mary of Bethany. Luke 10:42.
21. "Whatsoever thy hand findeth to do, do it with thy might." Eccl. 9:10.
22. The parable of the prodigal son. Luke 15:18.
23. "Whosoever shall give to drink unto one of these little ones a cup of cold water only in the name of a disciple, verily I say unto you, he shall in no wise lose his reward." Matt. 10:42.
24. "God is a Spirit: and they that worship him must worship him in spirit and in truth." John 4:24.
25. Jacob. Gen. 49:10.

## SERIES XXXIX

1. "Pure religion and undefiled before God and the Father is this, to visit the fatherless and widows in their affliction, and to keep himself unspotted from the world." Jas. 1:27.
2. "I thank thee, O Father, Lord of heaven and earth, because thou hast hid these things from the wise and prudent, and hast revealed them unto babes." Matt. 11:25.
3. Esau. Gen. 25:32.
4. "God is love." 1 John 4:8.
5. "Search me, O God, and know my heart: try me, and know my thoughts: and see if there be any wicked way in me, and lead me in the way everlasting." Ps. 139: 23, 24.
6. Peter, when brought before the Sanhedrin. Acts 4:12.
7. "From the rising of the sun even unto the going down of the same my name shall be great among the Gentiles." Mal. 1:11.
8. Jacob, of Reuben. Gen. 49:4.
9. Heb. 13:20, 21.
10. "Our Father which art in heaven," etc. Matt. 6:9-13.
11. "The word is very nigh unto thee, in thy mouth, and in thy heart, that thou mayest do it." Deut. 30:14.
12. "Lying lips are an abomination to the Lord: but they that deal truly are his delight." Prov. 13:22.
13. James, at the first church council. Acts 15:18.
14. Herod Agrippa I. Acts 12:22.
15. "Christ . . . who his own self bare our sins in his own body on the tree, that we, being dead to sins, should live unto righteousness: by whose stripes ye were healed." 1 Pet. 2:24.
16. "He [God] knoweth the way that I take: when he hath tried me, I shall come forth as gold." Job 23:10.
17. "This is my beloved Son, in whom I am well pleased; hear ye him." Matt. 17:5.
18. "They that are sick." Matt. 9:12.
19. "I am the way, the truth, and the life: no man cometh unto the Father, but by me." John 14:6.
20. "Casting all your care upon him [God]; for he careth for you." 1 Pet. 5:7.
21. "He that hath seen me hath seen the Father." John 14:9.

22. "Let not your heart be troubled: ye believe in God, believe also in me." John 14:1.
23. "When they deliver you up, take no thought how or what ye shall speak: for it shall be given you in that same hour what ye shall speak." Matt. 10:19.
24. "I am the bread of life: he that cometh to me shall never hunger; and he that believeth on me shall never thirst." John 6:35.
25. "The race is not to the swift, nor the battle to the strong." Eccl. 9: 11.

## SERIES XL

1. "He that will love life, and see good days, let him refrain his tongue from evil, and his lips that they speak no guile: let him eschew evil and do good; let him seek peace, and ensue it." 1 Pet. 3:10, 11.
2. "What doth the Lord require of thee, but to do justly, and to love mercy, and to walk humbly with thy God?" Micah 6:8.
3. "Come unto me, all ye that labor and are heavy laden, and I will give you rest." Matt. 11:28.
4. Jacob, at Bethel. Gen. 28:17.
5. "A double minded man is unstable in all his ways." Jas. 1:8.
6. "A false balance is abomination to the Lord: but a just weight is his delight." Prov. 11:1.
7. "My yoke is easy, and my burden is light." Matt. 11:30.
8. "Except the Lord build the house, they labor in vain that build it: except the Lord keep the city, the watchman waketh but in vain." Ps. 127:1.
9. Moses at the burning bush. Ex. 3:5.
10. Peter. Acts 10:34.
11. "The Lord seeth not as man seeth; for man looketh on the outward appearance, but the Lord looketh on the heart." 1 Sam. 16:7.
12. Of the Capernaum centurion. Matt. 8:10.

13. "Rejoice greatly, O daughter of Zion; shout, O daughter of Jerusalem: behold, thy King cometh unto thee: he is just, and having salvation; lowly, and riding upon an ass, and upon a colt the foal of an ass." Zech. 9:9.
14. To Paul. Corinth. Acts 18:10.
15. "Hereby do we know that we know him, if we keep his commandments." 1 John 2:3.
16. "These shall go away into everlasting punishment: but the righteous into life eternal." Matt. 25:46.
17. "I go to prepare a place for you." John 14:2.
18. Christ. Matt. 9:13.
19. "I will pray the Father, and he shall give you another Comforter, that he may abide with you forever; even the Spirit of truth." John 14: 16, 17.
20. "Ye are my friends, if ye do whatsoever I command you." John 15: 14.
21. "Faith, if it have not works, is dead, being alone." Jas. 2:17.
22. "Neither pray I for these alone, but for them also which shall believe on me through their word; that they all may be one." John 17:20, 21.
23. "Cast thy bread upon the waters: for thou shalt find it after many days." Eccl. 11:1.
24. "Feed my lambs." "Feed my sheep." John 21: 15-17.
25. "Fear not them which kill the body, but are not able to kill the soul: but rather fear him which is able to destroy both soul and body in hell." Matt. 10:28.

## SERIES XLI

1. "It is more blessed to give than to receive." Acts 20:35.
2. "Not that which goeth into the mouth defileth a man; but that which cometh out of the mouth, this defileth a man." Matt. 15:11.
3. "If the blind lead the blind, both shall fall into the ditch." Matt. 15:14.

4. "I have compassion on the multitude." Matt. 15:32.

5. "O ye hypocrites, ye can discern the face of the sky; but can ye not discern the signs of the times?" Matt. 16:3.

6. "Whosoever will save his life shall lose it: and whosoever will lose his life for my sake shall find it." Matt. 16:25.

7. "If ye have faith as a grain of mustard seed, ye shall say unto this mountain, Remove hence to yonder place; and it shall remove; and nothing shall be impossible unto you." Matt. 17:20.

8. "Whosoever therefore shall humble himself as this little child, the same is greatest in the kingdom of heaven." Matt. 18:4.

9. "Take heed that ye despise not one of these little ones; for I say unto you, That in heaven their angels do always behold the face of my Father which is in heaven." Matt. 18:10.

10. "Where two or three are gathered together in my name, there am I in the midst of them." Matt. 18:20.

11. "I say not unto thee, Until seven times: but, Until seventy times seven." Matt. 18:22.

12. "What therefore God hath joined together, let not man put asunder." Matt. 19:6.

13. "Suffer little children, and forbid them not, to come unto me: for of such is the kingdom of heaven." Matt. 19:14.

14. "All things, whatsoever ye shall ask in prayer, believing, ye shall receive." Matt. 21:22.

15. "He that shall endure unto the end, the same shall be saved." Matt. 24:13.

16. "Wheresoever the carcass is, there will the eagles be gathered together." Matt. 24:28.

17. "Because thou hast seen me, thou hast believed: blessed are they that have not seen, and yet have believed." John 20:29.

18. "Therefore be ye also ready: for in such an hour as ye think not the Son of man cometh." Matt. 24:44.

19. "Well done, good and faithful servant; thou hast been faithful over a few things, I will make thee ruler over many things: enter thou into the joy of thy Lord." Matt. 25:23.

20. "Inasmuch as ye have done it unto one of the least of these my brethren, ye have done it unto me." Matt. 25:40.

21. "Watch and pray, that ye enter not into temptation: the spirit indeed is willing, but the flesh is weak." Matt. 26:41.

22. "Put up again thy sword into his place: for all they that take the sword shall perish with the sword." Matt. 26:52.

23. "When they shall rise from the dead, they neither marry, nor are given in marriage; but are as the angels which are in heaven." Mark 12:25.

24. Of the poor widow who gave two mites—her all. Mark 12:43, 44.

25. "Ye shall be hated of all men for my name's sake: but he that shall endure unto the end, the same shall be saved." Mark 13:13.

26. "False Christs and false prophets shall rise, and shall show signs and wonders, to seduce, if it were possible, even the elect." Mark 13:22.

27. "Heaven and earth shall pass away: but my words shall not pass away." Mark 13:31.

28. "What I say unto you I say unto all, Watch." Mark 13:37.

29. "She hath done what she could: she is come aforehand to anoint my body to the burying." Mark 14:8.

30. "Verily I say unto thee, That this day, even in this night, before the cock crow twice, thou shalt deny me thrice." Mark 14:30.

31. "Launch out into the deep, and let down your nets for a draught." Luke 5:4.

32. "Fear not; from henceforth thou shalt catch men." Luke 5:10.

33. "Man, thy sins are forgiven thee." Luke 5:20.
34. "They that are whole need not a physician; but they that are sick." Luke 5:31.
35. "No man putteth new wine into old bottles [wine-skins]; else the new wine will burst the bottles, and be spilled, and the bottles shall perish." Luke 5:37.
36. "No man also having drunk old wine straightway desireth new: for he saith, The old is better." Luke 5:39.
37. "The Son of man is Lord also of the Sabbath." Luke 6:5.
38. "Woe unto you that are rich! for ye have received your consolation." Luke 6:24.
39. "Woe unto you, when all men shall speak well of you!" Luke 6:26.
40. "Give, and it shall be given unto you; good measure, pressed down, and shaken together, and running over, shall men give into your bosom. For with the same measure that ye mete withal it shall be measured to you again." Luke 6:38.
41. "Why call ye me, Lord, Lord, and do not the things which I say?" Luke 6:46.
42. "Young man, I say unto thee, Arise." Luke 7:14.
43. "Blessed is he, whosoever shall not be offended in me." Luke 7:23.
44. "Wisdom is justified of all her children." Luke 7:35.
45. "To whom little is forgiven, the same loveth little." Luke 7:47.
46. "Return to thine own house, and show how great things God hath done unto thee." Luke 8:39.
47. "If any man will come after me, let him deny himself, and take up his cross daily, and follow me." Luke 9:23.
48. "Whosoever shall be ashamed of me and of my words, of him shall the Son of man be ashamed, when he shall come in his own glory, and in his Father's, and of the holy angels." Luke 9:26.

49. "He that is not against us is for us." Luke 9:50.
50. "Let the dead bury their dead: but go thou and preach the kingdom of God." Luke 9:60.
51. "No man, having put his hand to the plough, and looking back, is fit for the kingdom of God." Luke 9:62.
52. "I beheld Satan as lightning fall from heaven." Luke 10:18.
53. "Go, and do thou likewise." Luke 10:37.
54. "He that is not with me is against me: and he that gathereth not with me scattereth." Luke 11:23.
55. "Whosoever he be of you that forsaketh not all that he hath, he cannot be my disciple." Luke 14:33.
56. "Joy shall be in heaven over one sinner that repenteth, more than over ninety and nine just persons, which need no repentance." Luke 15:7.
57. "The children of this world are in their generation wiser than the children of light." Luke 16:8.
58. "Make to yourselves friends of the mammon of unrighteousness; that, when ye fail, they may receive you into everlasting habitations." Luke 16:9.
59. "He that is faithful in that which is least is faithful also in much: and he that is unjust in the least is unjust also in much." Luke 16:10.
60. "Between us and you there is a great gulf fixed: so that they which would pass from hence to you cannot; neither can they pass to us, that would come from thence." Luke 16:26.
61. "Were there not ten cleansed? but where are the nine?" Luke 17:17.
62. "The kingdom of God cometh not with observation: neither shall they say, Lo here! or, lo there! for, behold, the kingdom of God is within you." Luke 17:21.
63. "Every one that exalteth himself shall be abased; and he that hum-

bleth himself shall be exalted." Luke 18:14.

64. "I have prayed for thee, that thy faith fail not: and when thou art converted, strengthen thy brethren." Luke 22:32.

65. "Pray that ye enter not into temptation." Luke 22:40.

66. "Father, forgive them; for they know not what they do." Luke 23:34.

67. "To-day shalt thou be with me in paradise." Luke 23:43.

68. "Father, into thy hands I commend my spirit." Luke 23:46.

69. "O fools, and slow of heart to believe all that the prophets have spoken: ought not Christ to have suffered these things, and to enter into his glory?" Luke 24:25, 26.

70. "Behold, I send the promise of my Father upon you: but tarry ye in the city of Jerusalem, until ye be endued with power from on high." Luke 24:49.

71. "Destroy this temple, and in three days I will raise it up." John 2:19.

72. "Except a man be born again, he cannot see the kingdom of God." John 3:3.

73. To Nicodemus. "As Moses lifted up the serpent in the wilderness, even so must the Son of man be lifted up: that whosoever believeth in him should not perish, but have everlasting life." John 3:14, 15.

74. "Whosoever drinketh of this water shall thirst again: but whosoever drinketh of the water that I shall give him shall never thirst; but the water that I shall give him shall be in him a well of water springing up into everlasting life." John 4: 13, 14.

75. "My meat is to do the will of him that sent me, and to finish his work." John 4:34.

76. "Lift up your eyes, and look on the fields; for they are white already to harvest." John 4:35.

77. "My Father worketh hitherto, and I work." John 5:17.

78. "Search the scriptures; for in them ye think ye have eternal life: and they are they which testify of me." John 5:39.

79. "Labor not for the meat which perisheth, but for that meat which endureth unto everlasting life, which the Son of man shall give unto you: for him hath God the Father sealed." John 6:27.

80. "This is the work of God, that ye believe on him whom he hath sent." John 6:29.

81. "He that eateth my flesh, and drinketh my blood, dwelleth in me, and I in him." John 6:56.

82. "If any man will do his will, he shall know of the doctrine, whether it be of God, or whether I speak of myself." John 7:17.

83. "If any man thirst, let him come unto me, and drink." John 7:37.

84. "He that is without sin among you, let him first cast a stone at her." John 8:7.

85. "I am the light of the world: he that followeth me shall not walk in darkness, but shall have the light of life." John 8:12.

86. "I, if I be lifted up from the earth, will draw all men unto me." John 12:32.

87. "If I then, your Lord and Master, have washed your feet; ye also ought to wash one another's feet." John 13:14.

88. "A new commandment I give unto you, That ye love one another; as I have loved you, that ye also love one another." John 13:34.

89. "He that believeth on me, the works that I do shall he do also; and greater works than these shall he do; because I go unto my Father." John 14:12.

90. "Because I live, ye shall live also." John 14:19.

91. "The Comforter, which is the Holy Ghost, whom the Father will send in my name, he shall teach you all things, and bring all things to your remembrance, whatsoever I have said unto you." John 14:26.

92. "Peace I leave with you, my peace

I give unto you: not as the world giveth, give I unto you." John 14:27.

93. "I am the vine, ye are the branches: He that abideth in me, and I in him, the same bringeth forth much fruit: for without me ye can do nothing." John 15:5.

94. "If ye abide in me, and my words abide in you, ye shall ask what ye will, and it shall be done unto you." John 15:7.

95. "Herein is my Father glorified, that ye bear much fruit; so shall ye be my disciples." John 15:8.

96. "These things have I spoken unto you, that my joy might remain in you, and that your joy might be full." John 15:11.

97. "When he is come, he will reprove the world of sin, and of righteousness, and of judgment." John 16:8.

98. "When he, the Spirit of truth, is come, he will guide you into all truth." John 16:13.

99. "Ask, and ye shall receive, that your joy may be full." John 16:24.

100. "In the world ye shall have tribulation: but be of good cheer; I have overcome the world." John 16:33.

101. "This is life eternal, that they might know thee the only true God, and Jesus Christ, whom thou hast sent." John 17:3.

## SERIES XLII

1. "Believe on the Lord Jesus Christ, and thou shalt be saved, and thy house." Acts 16:31.

2. "God that made the world and all things therein, seeing that he is Lord of heaven and earth, dwelleth not in temples made with hands." Acts 17:24.

3. "To be carnally minded is death; but to be spiritually minded is life and peace." Rom. 8:6.

4. "The fashion of this world passeth away." I Cor. 7:31.

5. "I am . . . a citizen of no mean city." Acts 21:39.

6. "Herein do I exercise myself, to have a conscience void of offence toward God, and toward men." Acts 24:16.

7. "I was not disobedient unto the heavenly vision." Said to King Agrippa II. Acts 26:19.

8. "This thing was not done in a corner." Said to Festus and Agrippa II. Acts 26:26.

9. When relating his vision on shipboard. Acts 27:23.

10. "As many as are led by the Spirit of God, they are the sons of God." Rom. 8:14.

11. "Heirs of God, and joint-heirs with Christ." Rom. 8:17.

12. "The Spirit also helpeth our infirmities: for we know not what we should pray for as we ought: but the Spirit itself maketh intercession for us with groanings which cannot be uttered." Rom. 8:26.

13. "We know that all things work together for good to them that love God, to them who are the called according to his purpose." Rom. 8:28.

14. "Whom he did foreknow, he also did predestinate to be conformed to the image of his Son, that he might be the firstborn among many brethren." Rom. 8:29.

15. "If God be for us, who can be against us?" Rom. 8:31.

16. "He that spared not his own Son, but delivered him up for us all, how shall he not with him also freely give us all things?" Rom. 8:32.

17. "Who shall separate us from the love of Christ? shall tribulation, or distress, or persecution, or famine, or nakedness, or peril, or sword?" Rom. 8:35.

18. "In all these things we are more than conquerors through him that loved us." Rom. 8:37.

19. "I am persuaded, that neither death, nor life, nor angels, nor principalities, nor powers, nor things present, nor things to come,

nor height, nor depth, nor any other creature, shall be able to separate us from the love of God, which is in Christ Jesus our Lord." Rom. 8:38, 39.

20. "O the depth of the riches both of the wisdom and knowledge of God! how unsearchable are his judgments, and his ways past finding out!" Rom. 11:33.

21. "I beseech you therefore, brethren, by the mercies of God, that ye present your bodies a living sacrifice, holy, acceptable unto God, which is your reasonable service." Rom. 12:1.

22. "Be not conformed to this world: but be ye transformed by the renewing of your mind, that ye may prove what is that good, and acceptable, and perfect, will of God." Rom. 12:2.

23. "For I say, through the grace given unto me, to every man that is among you, not to think of himself more highly than he ought to think: but to think soberly, according as God has dealt to every man the measure of faith." Rom. 12:3.

24. "We, being many, are one body in Christ, and every one members one of another." Rom. 12:5.

25. "Abhor that which is evil; cleave to that which is good." Rom. 12:9.

26. "Be kindly affectioned one to another with brotherly love; in honor preferring one another." Rom. 12:10.

27. "Not slothful in business; fervent in spirit; serving the Lord." Rom. 12:11.

28. "Rejoice with them that do rejoice, and weep with them that weep." Rom. 12:15.

29. "Recompense to no man evil for evil." Rom. 12:17.

30. "If it be possible, as much as lieth in you, live peaceably with all men." Rom. 12:18.

31. "If thine enemy hunger, feed him; if he thirst, give him drink: for in so doing thou shalt heap coals of fire on his head. Be not overcome of evil, but overcome evil with good." Rom. 12:20, 21.

32. "The powers that be are ordained of God." Rom. 13:1.

33. "Owe no man anything, but to love one another." Rom. 13:8.

34. "The night is far spent, the day is at hand: let us therefore cast off the works of darkness, and let us put on the armor of light." Rom. 13:12.

35. "Every one of us shall give account of himself to God." Rom. 14:12.

36. "The kingdom of God is not meat and drink; but righteousness, and peace, and joy in the Holy Ghost." Rom. 14:17.

37. "We then that are strong ought to bear the infirmities of the weak, and not to please ourselves." Rom. 15:1.

38. "Even Christ pleased not himself." Rom. 15:3.

39. "Whatsoever things were written aforetime were written for our learning, that we through patience and comfort of the scriptures might have hope." Rom. 15:4.

40. "I strived to preach the gospel, not where Christ was named, lest I should build upon another man's foundation." Rom. 15:20.

41. "The preaching of the cross is to them that perish foolishness; but unto us which are saved it is the power of God." 1 Cor. 1:18.

42. "Knowledge puffeth up, but charity edifieth." 1 Cor. 8:1.

43. "If any man think that he knoweth anything, he knoweth nothing yet as he ought to know." I Cor. 8:2.

44. "If meat make my brother to offend, I will eat no flesh while the world standeth, lest I make my brother to offend." 1 Cor. 8:13.

45. "Necessity is laid upon me; yea, woe is unto me, if I preach not the gospel!" 1 Cor. 9:16.

46. "I am made all things to all men, that I might by all means save some." 1 Cor. 9:22.

47. "Every man that striveth for the

mastery is temperate in all things. Now they do it to obtain a corruptible crown; but we an incorruptible." 1 Cor. 9:25.

48. "I keep under my body, and bring it into subjection: lest that by any means, when I have preached to others, I myself should be a castaway." 1 Cor. 9:27.

49. "Wherefore let him that thinketh he standeth take heed lest he fall." 1 Cor. 10:12.

50. "There hath no temptation taken you but such as is common to man: but God is faithful, who will not suffer you to be tempted above that ye are able; but will with the temptation also make a way to escape, that ye may be able to bear it." 1 Cor. 10:13.

51. "The cup of blessing which we bless, is it not the communion of the blood of Christ? The bread which we break, is it not the communion of the body of Christ?" 1 Cor. 10:16.

52. "Whether therefore ye eat, or drink, or whatsoever ye do, do all to the glory of God." 1 Cor. 10:31.

53. "As often as ye eat this bread, or drink this cup, ye do show the Lord's death till he come." 1 Cor. 11:26.

54. "If Christ be not risen, then is our preaching vain, and your faith is also vain." 1 Cor. 15:14.

55. "If in this life only we have hope in Christ, we are of all men most miserable." 1 Cor. 15:19.

56. "As in Adam all die, even so in Christ shall all be made alive." 1 Cor. 15:22.

57. "Be not deceived; evil communications corrupt good manners." 1 Cor. 15:33.

58. "It is sown in corruption; it is raised in incorruption: it is sown in dishonor; it is raised in glory: it is sown in weakness; it is raised in power: it is sown a natural body; it is raised a spiritual body." 1 Cor. 15:42-44.

59. "O death, where is thy sting: O grave, where is thy victory? The sting of death is sin; and the strength of sin is the law. But thanks be to God, which giveth us the victory through our Lord Jesus Christ." 1 Cor. 15:55-57.

60. "Therefore, my beloved brethren, be ye stedfast, unmoveable, always abounding in the work of the Lord, forasmuch as ye know that your labor is not in vain in the Lord." 1 Cor. 15:58.

61. "A great door and effectual is opened unto me, and there are many adversaries." 1 Cor. 16:9.

62. "Watch ye, stand fast in the faith, quit you like men, be strong." 1 Cor. 16:13.

63. "God was in Christ, reconciling the world unto himself, not imputing their trespasses unto them; and hath committed unto us the word of reconciliation." 2 Cor. 5:19.

64. "He hath made him to be sin for us, who knew no sin; that we might be made the righteousness of God in him." 2 Cor. 5:21.

65. "Be not unequally yoked together with unbelievers: for what fellowship hath righteousness with unrighteousness? and what communion hath light with darkness?" 2 Cor. 6:14.

66. "Come out from among them, and be ye separate, saith the Lord, and touch not the unclean thing; and I will receive you." 2 Cor. 6:17.

67. "We were troubled on every side; without were fightings, within were fears." 2 Cor. 7:5.

68. "Godly sorrow worketh repentance to salvation not to be repented of: but the sorrow of the world worketh death." 2 Cor. 7:10.

69. "Ye know the grace of our Lord Jesus Christ, that, though he was rich, yet for your sakes he became poor, that ye through his poverty might be rich." 2 Cor. 8:9.

70. "If there be first a willing mind, it is accepted according to that a man hath; and not according to that he hath not." 2 Cor. 8:12.

71. "Providing for honest things, not only in the sight of the Lord, but also in the sight of men." 2 Cor. 8:21.
72. "He which soweth sparingly shall reap also sparingly; and he which soweth bountifully shall reap also bountifully." 2 Cor. 9:6.
73. "Every man according as he purposeth in his heart, so let him give, not grudgingly, or of necessity: for God loveth a cheerful giver." 2 Cor. 9:7.
74. "Thanks be unto God for his unspeakable gift." 2 Cor. 9:15.
75. "Bringing into captivity every thought to the obedience of Christ." 2 Cor. 10:5.
76. "He that glorieth, let him glory in the Lord. For not he that commendeth himself is approved, but whom the Lord commendeth." 2 Cor. 10:17, 18.
77. "He said unto me, My grace is sufficient for thee: for my strength is made perfect in weakness." 2 Cor. 12:9.
78. "When I am weak, then am I strong." 2 Cor. 12:10.
79. "I will very gladly spend and be spent for you." 2 Cor. 12:15.
80. "In the mouth of two or three witnesses shall every word be established." 2 Cor. 13:1.
81. "The grace of the Lord Jesus Christ, and the love of God, and the communion of the Holy Ghost, be with you all. Amen." 2 Cor. 13:14.
82. "Save in the cross of our Lord Jesus Christ, by whom the world is crucified unto me, and I unto the world." Gal. 6:14.
83. "For his great love wherewith he loved us, even when we were dead in sins, hath quickened us together with Christ, (by grace ye are saved;) and hath raised us up together, and made us sit together in heavenly places in Christ Jesus." Eph. 2:4-6.
84. "By grace are ye saved through faith; and that not of yourselves:

it is the gift of God." Eph. 2:8.
85. "We are his workmanship, created in Christ Jesus unto good works, which God hath before ordained that we should walk in them." Eph. 2:10.
86. "Having no hope, and without God in the world." Eph. 2:12.
87. "He is our peace, who hath made both one, and hath broken down the middle wall of partition between us." Eph. 2:14.
88. "For this cause I bow my knees," etc. Eph. 3:14-19.
89. "Now unto him that is able to do exceeding abundantly above all that we ask or think, according to the power that worketh in us, unto him be glory in the church by Christ Jesus throughout all ages, world without end. Amen." Eph. 3:20, 21.
90. "Endeavoring to keep the unity of the Spirit in the bond of peace." Eph. 4:3.
91. "There is one body, and one Spirit, even as ye are called in one hope of your calling; one Lord, one faith, one baptism, one God and Father of all, who is above all, and through all, and in you all." Eph. 4:4-6.
92. "The measure of the stature of the fulness of Christ." Eph. 4:13.
93. "Speaking the truth in love." Eph. 4:15.
94. "Put on the new man, which after God is created in righteousness and true holiness." Eph. 4:24.
95. "Speak every man truth with his neighbor: for we are members one of another." Eph. 4:25.
96. "Be ye angry, and sin not: let not the sun go down upon your wrath." Eph. 4:26.
97. "Grieve not the Holy Spirit of God, whereby ye are sealed unto the day of redemption." Eph. 4:30.
98. "Be ye kind one to another, tenderhearted, forgiving one another, even as God for Christ's sake hath forgiven you." Eph. 4:32.
99. "Having a desire to depart, and to

be with Christ; which is far better." Phil. 1:23.

100. "Do all things without murmurings and disputings." Phil. 2:14.

101. "I count all things but loss for the excellency of the knowledge of Christ Jesus my Lord." Phil. 3:8.

102. "That I may know him, and the power of his resurrection, and the fellowship of his sufferings, being made conformable unto his death." Phil. 3:10.

103. "This one thing I do, forgetting those things which are behind, and reaching forth unto those things which are before, I press toward the mark for the prize of the high calling of God in Christ Jesus." Phil. 3:13, 14.

104. "Rejoice in the Lord alway: and again I say, rejoice." Phil. 4:4.

105. "Be careful for nothing; but in everything by prayer and supplication with thanksgiving let your requests be made known unto God." Phil. 4:6.

106. "The peace of God, which passeth all understanding, shall keep your hearts and minds through Christ Jesus." Phil. 4:7.

107. "Whatsoever things are true, whatsoever things are honest, whatsoever things are just, whatsoever things are pure, whatsoever things are lovely, whatsoever things are of good report; if there be any virtue, and if there be any praise, think on these things." Phil. 4:8.

108. "I have learned, in whatsoever state I am, therewith to be content." Phil. 4:11.

109. "I can do all things through Christ which strengtheneth me." Phil. 4:13.

110. "My God shall supply all your need according to his riches in glory by Christ Jesus." Phil. 4:19.

111. "According to his glorious power, unto all patience and longsuffering with joyfulness." Col. 1:11.

112. "He is before all things, and by him all things consist." Col. 1:17.

113. "In him dwelleth all the fulness of the Godhead bodily." Col. 2:9.

114. "Set your affection on things above, not on things on the earth." Col. 3:2.

115. "Let the word of Christ dwell in you richly in all wisdom; teaching and admonishing one another in psalms and hymns and spiritual songs, singing with grace in your hearts to the Lord." Col. 3:16.

116. "Walk in wisdom toward them that are without, redeeming the time." Col. 4:5.

117. "Let your speech be always with grace, seasoned with salt, that ye may know how ye ought to answer every man." Col. 4:6.

118. "God hath not given us the spirit of fear; but of power, and of love, and of a sound mind." 2 Tim. 1:7.

119. "I know whom I have believed, and am persuaded that he is able to keep that which I have committed unto him against that day." 2 Tim. 1:12.

120. "Thou therefore endure hardness, as a good soldier of Jesus Christ." 2 Tim. 2:3.

121. "No man that warreth entangleth himself with the affairs of this life; that he may please him who hath chosen him to be a soldier." 2 Tim. 2:4.

122. "Study to show thyself approved unto God, a workman that needeth not to be ashamed, rightly dividing the word of truth." 2 Tim. 2:15.

123. "The holy scriptures, which are able to make thee wise unto salvation through faith which is in Christ Jesus." 2 Tim. 3:15.

124. "All scripture is given by inspiration of God, and is profitable for doctrine, for reproof, for correction, for instruction in righteousness: that the man of God may be perfect, thoroughly furnished unto all good works." 2 Tim. 3:17.

125. "Preach the word: be instant in season, out of season." 2 Tim. 4:2.

126. "I have fought a good fight, I have

finished my course, I have kept the faith: henceforth there is laid up for me a crown of righteousness, which the Lord, the righteous judge, shall give me at that day: and not to me only, but unto all them also that love his appearing." 2 Tim. 4:8.

## SERIES XLIII

1. "Lift up your heads, O ye gates; and be ye lift up, ye everlasting doors, and the King of glory shall come in." Ps. 24:7.
2. "All the paths of the Lord are mercy and truth unto such as keep his covenant and testimonies." Ps. 25:10.
3. "The secret of the Lord is with them that fear him; and he will show them his covenant." Ps. 25:14.
4. "I will wash mine hands in innocency: so will I compass thine altar, O Lord." Ps. 26:6.
5. "Lord, I have loved the habitation of thy house, and the place where thine honor dwelleth." Ps. 26:8.
6. "The Lord is my light and my salvation; whom shall I fear? the Lord is the strength of my life; of whom shall I be afraid?" Ps. 27:1.
7. "One thing have I desired of the Lord, that will I seek after; that I may dwell in the house of the Lord all the days of my life, to behold the beauty of the Lord, and to enquire in his temple." Ps. 27:4.
8. "In the time of trouble he shall hide me in his pavilion: in the secret of his tabernacle shall he hide me; he shall set me up upon a rock." Ps. 27:5.
9. "When thou saidst, Seek ye my face, my heart said unto thee, Thy face, Lord, will I seek." Ps. 27:8.
10. "Why my father and my mother forsake me, then the Lord will take me up." Ps. 27:10.
11. "Wait on the Lord: be of good courage, and he shall strengthen thine heart: wait, I say, on the Lord." Ps. 27:14.

12. "Give unto the Lord the glory due unto his name: worship the Lord in the beauty of holiness." Ps. 29:2.
13. "The Lord will give strength unto his people; the Lord will bless his people with peace." Ps. 29:11.
14. "His anger endureth but a moment; in his favor is life: weeping may endure for a night, but joy cometh in the morning." Ps. 30:5.
15. "Be of good courage, and he shall strengthen thine heart, all ye that hope in the Lord." Ps. 31:24.
16. "Blessed is he whose transgression is forgiven, whose sin is covered. Blessed is the man unto whom the Lord imputeth not iniquity, and in whose spirit there is no guile." Ps. 32:1, 2.
17. "I acknowledged my sin unto thee, and mine iniquity have I not hid. I said, I will confess my transgressions unto the Lord, and thou forgavest the iniquity of my sin." Ps. 32:5.
18. "Thou art my hiding place; thou shalt preserve me from trouble; thou shalt compass me about with songs of deliverance." Ps. 32:7.
19. "I will instruct thee and teach thee in the way which thou shalt go: I will guide thee with mine eye." Ps. 32:8.
20. "Many sorrows shall be to the wicked: but he that trusteth in the Lord, mercy shall compass him about." Ps. 32:10.
21. "He loveth righteousness and judgment: the earth is full of the goodness of the Lord." Ps. 33:5.
22. "Blessed is the nation whose God is the Lord; and the people whom he hath chosen for his own inheritance." Ps. 33:12.
23. "Behold, the eye of the Lord is upon them that fear him, upon them that hope in his mercy." Ps. 33:18.
24. "I will bless the Lord at all times: his praise shall continually be in my mouth." Ps. 34:1.
25. "O magnify the Lord with me, and

let us exalt his name together."
Ps. 34:3.

26. "This poor man cried, and the Lord heard him, and saved him out of all his troubles." Ps. 34:6.

27. "The angel of the Lord encampeth round about them that fear him, and delivereth them." Ps. 34:7.

28. "O taste and see that the Lord is good: blessed is the man that trusteth in him." Ps. 34:8.

29. "O fear the Lord, ye his saints: for there is no want to them that fear him." Ps. 34:9.

30. "The young lions do lack, and suffer hunger: but they that seek the Lord shall not want any good thing." Ps. 34:10.

31. "Keep thy tongue from evil, and thy lips from speaking guile." Ps. 34:13.

32. "Depart from evil, and do good; seek peace, and pursue it." Ps. 34:14.

33. "The Lord is nigh unto them of a broken heart; and saveth such as be of a contrite spirit." Ps. 34:18.

34. "Many are the afflictions of the righteous: but the Lord delivereth him out of them all." Ps. 34:19.

35. "Thy mercy, O Lord, is in the heavens; and thy faithfulness reacheth unto the clouds." Ps. 36:5.

36. "How excellent is thy lovingkindness, O God! therefore the children of men put their trust under the shadow of thy wings." Ps. 36:7.

37. "With thee is the fountain of life: in thy light shall we see light." Ps. 36:9.

38. "Fret not thyself because of evildoers, neither be thou envious against the workers of iniquity." Ps. 37:1.

39. "Trust in the Lord, and do good; so shalt thou dwell in the land, and verily thou shalt be fed." Ps. 37:3.

40. "Delight thyself also in the Lord; and he shall give thee the desires of thine heart." Ps. 37:4.

41. "Commit thy way unto the Lord; trust also in him; and he shall bring it to pass." Ps. 37:5.

42. "The meek shall inherit the earth; and shall delight themselves in the abundance of peace." Ps. 37:11.

43. "A little that a righteous man hath is better than the riches of many wicked." Ps. 37:16.

44. "The steps of a good man are ordered by the Lord: and he delighteth in his way." Ps. 37:23.

45. "I have been young, and now am old; yet have I not seen the righteous forsaken, nor his seed begging bread." Ps. 37:25.

46. "I have seen the wicked in great power, and spreading himself like a green bay tree. Yet he passed away, and, lo, he was not: yea, I sought him, but he could not be found." Ps. 37:35, 36.

47. "Mark the perfect man, and behold the upright: for the end of that man is peace." Ps. 37:37.

48. "Lord, make me to know mine end, and the measure of my days, what it is; that I may know how frail I am." Ps. 39:4.

49. "Blessed is he that considereth the poor: the Lord will deliver him in time of trouble." Ps. 41:1.

50. "As the hart panteth after the water brooks, so panteth my soul after thee, O God." Ps. 42:1.

51. "Why art thou cast down, O my soul? and why art thou disquieted in me? hope thou in God: for I shall yet praise him for the help of his countenance." Ps. 42:5.

52. "O send out thy light and thy truth: let them lead me; let them bring me unto thy holy hill, and to thy tabernacles." Ps. 43:3.

53. "We have heard with our ears, O God, our fathers have told us, what work thou didst in their days, in the times of old." Ps. 44:1.

54. "God is our refuge and strength, a very present help in trouble. Therefore will we not fear, though the earth be removed, and though

the mountains be carried into the midst of the sea." Ps. 46:1, 2.

55. "He maketh wars to cease unto the end of the earth; he breaketh the bow, and cutteth the spear in sunder; he burneth the chariot in the fire." Ps. 46:9.

56. "Be still, and know that I am God: I will be exalted among the heathen, I will be exalted in the earth." Ps. 46:10.

57. "Walk about Zion, and go round about her: tell the towers thereof. Mark ye well her bulwarks, consider her palaces; that ye may tell it to the generation following." Ps. 48:12, 13.

58. "For this God is our God for ever and ever: he will be our guide even unto death." Ps. 48:14.

59. "A day in thy courts is better than a thousand. I had rather be a doorkeeper in the house of my God, than to dwell in the tents of wickedness." Ps. 84:10.

60. "The Lord is a sun and shield: the Lord will give grace and glory. No good thing will he withhold from them that walk uprightly." Ps. 84:11.

61. "Mercy and truth are met together; righteousness and peace have kissed each other." Ps. 85:10.

62. "Lord, thou hast been our dwellingplace in all generations. Before the mountains were brought forth, or ever thou hadst formed the earth and the world, even from everlasting to everlasting, thou art God." Ps. 90:1, 2.

63. "A thousand years in thy sight are but as yesterday when it is past, and as a watch in the night." Ps. 90:4.

64. "Thou hast set our iniquities before thee, our secret sins in the light of thy countenance." Ps. 90:8.

65. "The days of our years are threescore years and ten; and if by reason of strength they be fourscore years, yet it is their strength labor and sorrow; for it is soon cut off, and we fly away." Ps. 90:10.

66. "So teach us to number our days, that we may apply our hearts unto wisdom." Ps. 90:12.

67. "Let the beauty of the Lord our God be upon us: and establish thou the work of our hands upon us; yea, the work of our hands establish thou it." Ps. 90:17.

68. That he "shall abide under the shadow of the Almighty." Ps. 91:1.

69. "I will say of the Lord, He is my refuge and my fortress: my God, in him will I trust." Ps. 91:2.

70. "And ten thousand at thy right hand; but it shall not come nigh thee." Ps. 91:7.

71. "He shall give his angels charge over thee, to keep thee in all thy ways." Ps. 91:11.

72. "The Lord is clothed with strength, wherewith he hath girded himself: the world also is stablished, that it cannot be moved." Ps. 93:1.

73. "He that planted the ear, shall he not hear? he that formed the eye, shall he not see?" Ps. 94:9.

74. "O come, let us sing unto the Lord: let us make a joyful noise to the rock of our salvation." Ps. 95:1.

75. "O come, let us worship and bow down: let us kneel before the Lord our maker." Ps. 95:6.

76. "O sing unto the Lord a new song: sing unto the Lord, all the earth." Ps. 96:1.

77. "Declare his glory among the heathen, his wonders among all people. For the Lord is great, and greatly to be praised: he is to be feared above all gods. For all the gods of the nations are idols, but the Lord made the heavens." Ps. 96:3-5.

78. "O worship the Lord in the beauty of holiness: fear before him, all the earth." Ps. 96:9.

79. "What shall I render unto the Lord for all his benefits toward me? I will take the cup of salvation, and call upon the name of the

Lord. I will pay my vows unto the Lord now in the presence of all his people." Ps. 116:12-14.

80. "Precious in the sight of the Lord is the death of his saints." Ps. 116:15.

81. "And is become my salvation." Ps. 118:14.

82. That is "is become the head stone of the corner." Ps. 118:22.

83. "This is the day which the Lord hath made; we will rejoice and be glad in it." Ps. 118:24.

84. "Set a watch, O Lord, before my mouth; keep the door of my lips." Ps. 141:3.

85. "Lord, what is man, that thou takest knowledge of him! or the son of man, that thou makest account of him!" Ps. 144:3.

86. "I will extol thee, my God, O King; and I will bless thy name forever and ever. Every day will I bless thee; and I will praise thy name forever and ever." Ps. 145: 1, 2.

87. "The Lord is gracious, and full of compassion; slow to anger, and of great mercy. The Lord is good to all: and his tender mercies are over all his works." Ps. 145:8, 9.

88. "And satisfiest the desire of every living thing." Ps. 145:16.

89. "The Lord is righteous in all his ways, and holy in all his works." Ps. 145:17.

90. "The Lord is nigh unto all them that call upon him, to all that call upon him in truth." Ps. 145:18.

91. "Praise ye the Lord: for it is good to sing praises unto our God; for it is pleasant; and praise is comely." Ps. 147:1.

92. "He healeth the broken in heart, and bindeth up their wounds." Ps. 147:3.

93. "He maketh peace in thy borders, and filleth thee with the finest of the wheat." Ps. 147:14.

### SERIES XLIV.

1. "There is that maketh himself rich, yet hath nothing: there is that maketh himself poor, yet hath great riches." Prov. 13:7.

2. "Hope deferred maketh the heart sick." Prov. 13:12.

3. "He that spareth his rod hateth his son: but he that loveth him chasteneth him betimes." Prov. 13:24.

4. "The heart knoweth his own bitterness." Prov. 14:10.

5. "There is a way which seemeth right unto a man, but the end thereof are the ways of death." Prov. 14:12.

6. "In all labor there is profit: but the talk of the lips tendeth only to penury." Prov. 14:23.

7. "Righteousness exalteth a nation, but sin is a reproach to any people." Prov. 14:34.

8. "A soft answer turneth away wrath: but grievous words stir up anger." Prov. 15:1.

9. "Proud and haughty scorner is his name, who dealeth in proud wrath." Prov. 21:24.

10. "A good name is rather to be chosen than great riches, and loving favor rather than silver and gold." Prov. 22:1.

11. "The rich and poor meet together: the Lord is the maker of them all." Prov. 22:2.

12. "A prudent man forseeth the evil, and hideth himself: but the simple pass on, and are punished." Prov. 22:3.

13. "Train up a child in the way he should go: and when he is old, he will not depart from it." Prov. 22:6.

14. "The borrower is servant to the lender." Prov. 22:7.

15. "There is a lion without, I shall be slain in the streets." Prov. 22:13.

16. "Remove not the ancient landmark, which thy fathers have set." Prov. 22:28.

17. "Seest thou a man diligent in his business? he shall stand before kings; he shall not stand before mean men." Prov. 22:29.

18. "Riches certainly make themselves wings; they fly away as an eagle

toward heaven." Prov. 23:5.

19. "As he thinketh in his heart, so is he." Prov. 23:7.

20. "The drunkard and the glutton shall come to poverty: and drowsiness shall clothe a man with rags." Prov. 23:21.

21. "At the last it biteth like a serpent, and stingeth like an adder." Prov. 23:32.

22. "Every man shall kiss his lips that giveth a right answer." Prov. 24:26.

23. "Yet a little sleep, a little slumber, a little folding of the hands to sleep: so shall thy poverty come as one that travelleth; and thy want as an armed man." Prov. 24:33, 34.

24. "A word fitly spoken is like apples of gold in pictures of silver." Prov. 25:11.

25. "If thine enemy be hungry, give him bread to eat; and if he be thirsty, give him water to drink: for thou shalt heap coals of fire upon his head, and the Lord shall reward thee." Prov. 25:21, 22.

26. "As cold waters to a thirsty soul, so is good news from a far country." Prov. 25:25.

27. "Answer not a fool according to his folly, lest thou also be like unto him. Answer a fool according to his folly, lest he be wise in his own conceit." Prov. 26:4, 5.

28. "Seest thou a man wise in his own conceit? there is more hope of a fool than of him." Prov. 26:12.

29. "Where no wood is, there the fire goeth out: so where there is no talebearer, the strife ceaseth." Prov. 26:20.

30. "Boast not thyself of to-morrow; for thou knowest not what a day may bring forth." Prov. 27:1.

31. "Let another man praise thee, and not thine own mouth; a stranger, and not thine own lips." Prov. 27:2.

32. "Faithful are the wounds of a friend; but the kisses of an enemy are deceitful." Prov. 27:6.

33. "Iron sharpeneth iron; so a man sharpeneth the countenance of his friend." Prov. 27:17.

34. "The wicked flee when no man pursueth: but the righteous are bold as a lion." Prov. 28:1.

35. "A fool uttereth all his mind: but a wise man keepeth it in till afterwards." Prov. 29:11.

36. "Where there is no vision, the people perish: but he that keepeth the law, happy is he." Prov. 29:18.

37. "Seest thou a man that is hasty in his words? there is more hope of a fool than of him." Prov. 29:20.

38. "Remove far from me vanity and lies: give me neither poverty nor riches; feed me with food convenient for me." Prov. 30:8.

39. "Who can find a virtuous woman? for her price is far above rubies." Prov. 31:10.

40. "Favor is deceitful, and beauty is vain: but a woman that feareth the Lord, she shall be praised." Prov. 31:30.

## SERIES XLV

1. "Shall the axe boast itself against him that heweth therewith? or shall the saw magnify itself against him that shaketh it?" Isa. 10:15.

2. "There shall come forth a rod out of the stem of Jesse, and a Branch shall grow out of his roots." Isa. 11:1.

3. "The spirit of the Lord shall rest upon him, the spirit of wisdom and understanding, the spirit of counsel and might, the spirit of knowledge and of the fear of the Lord." Isa. 11:2.

4. "With righteousness shall he judge the poor, and reprove with equity for the meek of the earth: and he shall smite the earth with the rod of his mouth, and with the breath of his lips shall he slay the wicked." Isa. 11:4.

5. "The wolf also shall dwell with the lamb, and the leopard shall lie

down with the kid; and the calf and the young lion and the fatling together; and a little child shall lead them." Isa. 11:6.

6. "The earth shall be full of the knowledge of the Lord, as the waters cover the sea." Isa. 11:9.

7. "Behold, God is my salvation; I will trust, and not be afraid: for the Lord Jehovah is my strength and my song; he also is become my salvation. Therefore with joy shall ye draw water out of the wells of salvation." Isa. 12:2, 3.

8. "How art thou fallen from heaven, O Lucifer, son of the morning! how art thou cut down to the ground, which didst weaken the nations!" Isa. 14:12.

9. "Thou wilt keep him in perfect peace, whose mind is stayed on thee: because he trusteth in thee." Isa. 26:3.

10. "Trust ye in the Lord forever: for in the Lord Jehovah is everlasting strength." Isa. 26:4.

11. "Woe to the crown of pride, to the drunkards of Ephraim, whose glorious beauty is a fading flower, which are on the head of the fat valleys of them that are overcome with wine!" Isa. 28:1.

12. "They also have erred through wine, and through strong drink are out of the way; the priest and the prophet have erred through strong drink, they are swallowed up of wine, they are out of the way through strong drink; they err in vision, they stumble in judgment." Isa. 28:7.

13. "Precept must be upon precept, precept upon precept; line upon line, line upon line; here a little, and there a little." Isa. 28:10.

14. "Behold I lay in Zion for a foundation a stone, a tried stone, a precious cornerstone; he that believeth shall not make haste." Isa. 28:16.

15. "The bed is shorter than that a man can stretch himself on it: and the covering narrower than that he can wrap himself in it." Isa. 28:20.

16. "In returning and rest shall ye be saved; in quietness and in confidence shall be your strength." Isa. 30:15.

17. "A man shall be as an hiding place from the wind, and a covert from the tempest; as rivers of water in a dry place, as the shadow of a great rock in a weary land." Isa. 32:2.

18. "The liberal deviseth liberal things, and by liberal things shall he stand." Isa. 32:8.

19. "The work of righteousness shall be peace; and the effect of righteousness quietness and assurance forever." Isa. 32:17.

20. "Blessed are ye that sow beside all waters, that send forth thither the feet of the ox and the ass." Isa. 32:20.

21. "He shall dwell on high: his place of defence shall be the munitions of rocks: bread shall be given him; his waters shall be sure." Isa. 33:16.

22. "Thine eyes shall see the king in his beauty: they shall behold the land that is very far off." Isa. 33:17.

23. "The wilderness and the solitary place shall be glad for them; and the desert shall rejoice, and blossom as the rose." Isa. 35:1.

24. "Strengthen ye the weak hands, and confirm the feeble knees. Say to them that are of a feeble heart, Be strong, fear not: behold, your God will come with vengeance, even God with a recompence; he will come and save you." Isa. 35:3, 4.

25. "Then the eyes of the blind shall be opened, and the ears of the deaf shall be unstopped. Then shall the lame man leap as an hart, and the tongue of the dumb sing: for in the wilderness shall waters break out, and streams in the desert." Isa. 35:5, 6.

26. "An highway shall be there, and a way, and it shall be called The

way of holiness; the unclean shall not pass over it; but it shall be for those: the wayfaring men, though fools, shall not err therein." Isa. 35:8.

27. "The ransomed of the Lord shall return, and come to Zion with songs and everlasting joy upon their heads: they shall obtain joy and gladness, and sorrow and sighing shall flee away." Isa. 35: 10.

28. "The remnant that is escaped of the house of Judah shall again take root downward and bear fruit upward." Isa. 37:31.

29. "Comfort ye, comfort ye, my people, saith your God. Speak ye comfortably to Jerusalem, and cry unto her, that her warfare is accomplished, that her iniquity is pardoned: for she hath received of the Lord's hand double for all her sins." Isa. 40:1, 2.

30. "Every valley shall be exalted, and every mountain and hill shall be made low: and the crooked shall be made straight, and the rough places plain." Isa. 40:4.

31. "The grass withereth, the flower fadeth: but the word of our God shall stand forever." Isa. 40:8.

32. "He shall feed his flock like a shepherd: he shall gather the lambs with his arm, and carry them in his bosom, and shall gently lead those that are with young." Isa. 40:11.

33. "Who hath measured the waters in the hollow of his hand, and meted out heaven with the span, and comprehended the dust of the earth in a measure, and weighed the mountains in scales, and the hills in a balance?" Isa. 40:12.

34. "Hast thou not known? hast thou not heard, that the everlasting God, the Lord, the Creator of the ends of the earth, fainteth not, neither is weary? There is no searching of his understanding." Isa. 40:28.

35. "He giveth power to the faint; and

to them that have no might he increaseth strength." Isa. 40:29.

36. "They that wait upon the Lord shall renew their strength; they shall mount up with wings as eagles; they shall run, and not be weary; and they shall walk, and not faint." Isa. 40:31.

37. "They helped every one his neighbor; and every one said to his brother, Be of good courage." Isa. 41:6.

38. "Be not dismayed; for I am thy God: I will strengthen thee; yea, I will help thee; yea, I will uphold thee with the right hand of my righteousness." Isa. 41: 10.

39. "For I the Lord thy God will hold thy right hand, saying unto thee, Fear not; I will help thee." Isa. 41:13.

40. "His visage was so marred more than any man, and his form more than the sons of men." Isa. 52:14.

41. "He hath no form nor comeliness; and when we shall see him, there is no beauty that we should desire him." Isa. 53:2.

42. "He is despised and rejected of men; a man of sorrows and acquainted with grief: and we hid as it were our faces from him; he was despised, and we esteemed him not." Isa. 53:3.

43. "Surely he hath borne our griefs, and carried our sorrows: yet we did esteem him stricken, smitten of God, and afflicted. But he was wounded for our transgressions, he was bruised for our iniquities: the chastisement of our peace was upon him; and with his stripes we are healed. All we like sheep have gone astray; we have turned every one to his own way; and the Lord hath laid on him the iniquity of us all." Isa. 53:4-6.

44. "He was oppressed, and he was afflicted, yet he opened not his mouth: he is brought as a lamb to the slaughter, and as a sheep before her shearers is dumb, so he openeth not his mouth." Isa. 53:7.

45. "He made his grave with the wicked, and with the rich in his death." Isa. 53:9.
46. "Enlarge the place of thy tent, and let them stretch forth the curtains of thine habitations: spare not, lengthen thy cords, and strengthen thy stakes." Isa. 54:2.
47. "The mountains shall depart, and the hills be removed; but my kindness shall not depart from thee, neither shall the covenant of my peace be removed, saith the Lord that hath mercy on thee." Isa. 54:10.
48. "All thy children shall be taught of the Lord; and great shall be the peace of thy children." Isa. 54:13.
49. "Ho, every one that thirsteth, come ye to the waters, and he that hath no money; come ye, buy, and eat; yea, come, buy wine and milk without money and without price." Isa. 55:1.
50. "Wherefore do ye spend money for that which is not bread? and your labor for that which satisfieth not? hearken diligently unto me, and eat ye that which is good, and let your soul delight itself in fatness." Isa. 55:2.
51. "Incline your ear, and come unto me: hear, and your soul shall live; and I will make an everlasting covenant with you, even the sure mercies of David." Isa. 55:3.
52. "Seek ye the Lord while he may be found, call ye upon him while he is near." Isa. 55:6.
53. "Let the wicked forsake his way, and the unrighteous man his thoughts: and let him return unto the Lord, and he will have mercy upon him; and to our God, for he will abundantly pardon." Isa. 55:7.
54. "My thoughts are not your thoughts, neither are your ways my ways, saith the Lord. For as the heavens are higher than the earth, so are my ways higher than your ways, and my thoughts than your thoughts." Isa. 55:8, 9.
55. "As the rain cometh down, and the snow from heaven, and returneth not thither, but watereth the earth, and maketh it bring forth and bud, that it may give seed to the sower, and bread to the eater: so shall my word be that goeth forth out of my mouth: it shall not return unto me void, but it shall accomplish that which I please, and it shall prosper in the thing whereto I sent it." Isa. 55:10, 11.
56. "Thus saith the high and lofty One that inhabiteth eternity, whose name is Holy; I dwell in the high and holy place, with him also that is of a contrite and humble spirit, to revive the spirit of the humble, and to revive the heart of the contrite ones." Isa. 57:15.
57. "The wicked are like the troubled sea, when it cannot rest, whose waters cast up mire and dirt. There is no peace, saith my God, to the wicked." Isa. 57:20, 21.
58. "Is not this the fast that I have chosen? to loose the bands of wickedness, to undo the heavy burdens, and to let the oppressed go free, and that ye break every yoke?" Isa. 58:6.
59. "If thou turn away thy foot from the Sabbath, from doing thy pleasure on my holy day; and call the Sabbath a delight, the holy of the Lord, honorable; and shalt honor him, not doing thine own ways, nor finding thine own pleasure, nor speaking thine own words: then shalt thou delight thyself in the Lord; and I will cause thee to ride upon the high places of the earth, and feed thee with the heritage of Jacob thy father: for the mouth of the Lord hath spoken it." Isa. 58:13, 14.
60. "Behold, the Lord's hand is not shortened, that it cannot save; neither his ear heavy, that it cannot hear: but your iniquities have separated between you and your God, and your sins have hid his face from you, that he will not hear." Isa. 59:1, 2.

61. "Arise, shine; for thy light is come, and the glory of the Lord is risen upon thee." Isa. 60:1.

62. "The Gentiles shall come to thy light, and kings to the brightness of thy rising." Isa. 60:3.

63. "The nation and kingdom that will not serve thee shall perish; yea, those nations shall be utterly wasted." Isa. 60:12.

64. "Thou shalt call thy walls Salvation, and thy gates Praise." Isa. 60:18.

65. "The sun shall be no more thy light by day; neither for brightness shall the moon give light unto thee: but the Lord shall be unto thee an everlasting light, and thy God thy glory." Isa. 60:19.

66. "Thy sun shall no more go down; neither shall thy moon withdraw itself: for the Lord shall be thine everlasting light, and the days of thy mourning shall be ended." Isa. 60:20.

67. "A little one shall become a thousand, and a small one a strong nation: I the Lord will hasten it in his time." Isa. 60:22.

68. "The Spirit of the Lord God is upon me; because the Lord hath anointed me to preach good tidings unto the meek; he hath sent me to bind up the brokenhearted, to proclaim liberty to the captives, and the opening of the prison to them that are bound; to proclaim the acceptable year of the Lord." Isa. 61:1, 2.

69. "And the day of vengeance of our God; to comfort all that mourn; to appoint unto them that mourn in Zion, to give unto them beauty for ashes, the oil of joy for mourning, the garment of praise for the spirit of heaviness; that they might be called trees of righteousness, the planting of the Lord, that he might be glorified." Isa. 61:2, 3.

70. "I have set watchmen upon thy walls, O Jerusalem, which shall never hold their peace day nor night: ye that make mention of the Lord, keep not silence." Isa. 62:6.

71. "I have trodden the winepress alone; and of the people there was none with me." Isa. 63:3.

72. "In all their affliction he was afflicted." Isa. 63:9.

73. "We are the clay, and thou our potter; and we all are the work of thy hand." Isa. 64:8.

74. "They shall teach no more every man his neighbor, and every man his brother, saying, Know the Lord: for they shall all know me, from the least of them unto the greatest of them, saith the Lord: for I will forgive their iniquity, and I will remember their sin no more." Jer. 31:34.

75. "Seekest thou great things for thyself? seek them not." Jer. 45:5.

76. "Is it nothing to you, all ye that pass by? behold, and see if there be any sorrow like unto my sorrow." Lam. 1:12.

77. "They are new every morning: great is thy faithfulness." Lam. 3:23.

78. "It is good for a man that he bear the yoke in his youth." Lam. 3:27.

79. "The lion hath roared, who will not fear? the Lord God hath spoken, who can but prophesy?" Amos 3:8.

80. "Prepare to meet thy God, O Israel." Amos 4:12.

81. "Ye who turn judgment to wormwood, and leave off righteousness in the earth." Amos 5:7.

82. "Seek him that maketh the seven stars and Orion, and turneth the shadow of death into the morning, and maketh the day dark with night: that calleth for the waters of the sea, and poureth them out upon the face of the earth: The Lord is his name." Amos 5:8.

83. "They hate him that rebuketh in the gate, and they abhor him that speaketh uprightly." Amos 5:10.

84. "Forasmuch therefore as your treading is upon the poor, and ye take from him burdens of wheat: ye have built houses of hewn

stone, but ye shall not dwell in them; ye have planted pleasant vineyards, but ye shall not drink wine of them." Amos 5:11.

85. "Hate the evil, and love the good, and establish judgment in the gate: it may be that the Lord God of hosts will be gracious unto the remnant of Joseph." Amos 5:15.

86. "Let judgment run down as waters, and righteousness as a mighty stream." Amos 5:24.

87. "Woe to them that are at ease in Zion, and trust in the mountain of Samaria!" Amos 6:1.

88. "I was no prophet, neither was I a prophet's son; but I was an herdman, and a gatherer of sycomore fruit: and the Lord took me as I followed the flock, and the Lord said unto me, Go, prophesy unto my people Israel." Amos 7: 14, 15.

89. Jonah. Jonah 4:8.

90. That about beating swords into plowshares. Isa. 2:4; Mic. 4:3.

91. "They shall sit every man under his vine and under his fig tree; and none shall make them afraid." Mic. 4:4.

92. "But thou, Beth-lehem Ephratah, though thou be little among the thousands of Judah, yet out of thee shall he come forth unto me that is to be ruler in Israel; whose goings forth have been from of old, from everlasting." Mic. 5:2.

93. "Return unto me, and I will return unto you, saith the Lord of hosts." Mal. 3:7.

94. "Will a man rob God? Yet ye have robbed me. But ye say, Wherein have we robbed ye? In tithes and offerings." Mal. 3:8.

95. "Bring ye all the tithes into the storehouse, that there may be meat in mine house, and prove me now herewith, saith the Lord of hosts, if I will not open you the windows of heaven, and pour you out a blessing, that there shall not be room enough to receive it." Mal. 3:10.

96. "Then they that feared the Lord spoke often one to another: and the Lord hearkened, and heard it, and a book of remembrance was written before him for them that feared the Lord, and that thought upon his name." Mal. 3:16.

97. "They shall be mine, saith the Lord of hosts, in that day when I make up my jewels; and I will spare them, as a man spareth his own son that serveth him." Mal. 3:17.

98. "Unto you that fear my name shall the Sun of righteousness arise with healing in his wings; and ye shall go forth, and grow up as calves of the stall." Mal. 4:2.

99. "Behold, I will send you Elijah the prophet before the coming of the great and dreadful day of the Lord." Mal. 4:5.

100. "And he shall turn the heart of the fathers to the children, and the heart of the children to their fathers, lest I come and smite the earth with a curse." Mal. 4:6.